Fascinating Foods from the Deep South

Alline Van Duzor marks the spot for a tree planting on Greensboro Avenue in downtown Tuscaloosa in the late 1950s, as part of a civic beautification effort. Courtesy of The University Club.

Fascinating Foods from the Deep South

Favorite Recipes from the University Club of Tuscaloosa, Alabama

Alline P. Van Duzor

Foreword by Camille Maxwell Elebash

Fire Ant Books

∞

The paper on which this book is printed meets the minimum requirements of American National Standard for Information Sciences-Permanence of Paper for Printed Library Materials, ANSI Z39.48-1984.

Library of Congress Cataloging-in-Publication Data

Van Duzor, Alline P.
Fascinating foods from the Deep South : favorite recipes from the University Club of Tuscaloosa, Alabama / Alline P. Van Duzor.
p. cm.
"Fire Ant books."
Includes index.
ISBN 978-0-8173-5638-5 (pbk. : alk. paper) 1. Cookery, American—Southern style. 2. University Club of Tuscaloosa, Alabama. I. Title.
TX715.V28 2010
641.5975—dc22

2010000259

Contents

	Frontispiece	ii
	Guide to Portions and Brand Name Foods	vii
	Foreword by Camille Maxwell Elebash	ix
I.	Beverages	1
II.	Breads	5
	Baking Powder	7
	Yeast	11
	Miscellaneous	13
III.	Cakes and Cake Frostings	15
	Cakes	17
	Cake Frostings and Fillings	20
IV.	Cheese Dishes	23
V.	Cookies	27
VI.	Desserts (See also section entitled "Pies & Tarts")	33
	Chocolate	35
	Non-Chocolate	37
VII.	Eggs	45
VIII.	Meat Cookery	49
IX.	Pies and Tarts	57
	Pastries and Shells	59
	Pies	59
	Chiffon Pies	62
	Tarts	64

X. Poultry 67

XI. Salads and Salad Dressings 75

Salads 77

Salad Dressings 82

XII. Sauces 83

For Desserts 85

For Meat and Vegetables 86

XIII. Seafoods 89

XIV. Soups 95

XV. Vegetables 99

XVI. Miscellaneous 109

XVII. New Recipes 113

Appendix: Presidents of the University Club 119

Index 121

Guide to Portions and Brand Name Foods

Canned food sizes:

Canned food sizes:

#1 can = 1¼ cups or 10 to 12 oz.

#2 can = 20 oz. or 17½ fl. oz.

#2½ can = 28 to 30 oz.

#3 can = 51 oz.

#10 can = 98 to 117 oz. or 6¼ to 7¼ lbs.

#303 can = 2 cups or 16 to 17 oz.

Brand name ingredients:

A & P Angel Food Cake: A & P supermarkets were once a national chain, but are now concentrated in New York City, New Jersey, and Connecticut. Any quality supermarket angel food cake will work as a substitute.

Baker's chocolate, Baker's bitter chocolate, Baker's unsweetened cocoa: still available under slightly different names (e.g., bittersweet and unsweetened chocolate). Modern cooks should remember that over time the cocoa bean content of "chocolate" has decreased and should adapt portions accordingly.

Borden's Vera-Sharp Cheese: a pasteurized cheddar-flavored cheese spread also sold in slices for sandwiches and as an adjunct to apple pie.

Campbell's Tomato Soup: has changed little since its debut in 1897.

Coca Cola: a standard 12-ounce can or bottle of original Coke.

Hershey's 10-cent chocolate bar: Hershey did not introduce the 10-

cent bar until 1969. Van Duzor probably meant the 5-cent bar, which in 1960 contained 1 oz. of chocolate. Again, modern cooks should remember that the cocoa bean content of "chocolate" has decreased and should adapt portions accordingly.

India Relish: now a brand variety sold by Heinz, this relish has been described as a cross between chow chow and sweet pickle relish.

Kellogg's All Bran: wheat bran cereal.

Lea & Perrins: Worcestershire sauce.

Philadelphia Cream Cheese: the "small packages" cited in the recipes were probably 3 oz.

Royal Anne cherries: canned Royal Anne cherries are available from Oregon Foods.

Shefford's Snappy Cheese: Van Duzor was probably working from an older favorite recipe, as this brand of cheese was not manufactured after 1946. It was a direct competitor to Borden's Vera-Sharp, a cheddar-flavor spreadable pasteurized cheese.

XXXX sugar: confectioners' sugar.

Foreword

In the early years of the University Club, the major force behind the gracious dining in that elegant antebellum house was Alline Van Duzor, who presided over the club with a will as strong as the cast-iron skillets that hung in the kitchen. From that kitchen emerged mouth-watering southern cuisine, served by a loyal and efficient staff to a generation of University and Tuscaloosa people.

Louise Faircloth, who was the only female member of the club board in those early years, remembers that Neige Todhunter, dean of what was then called the School of Home Economics, recommended Van Duzor to manage the club. Faircloth became a staunch supporter of Van Duzor's employment and points with pride to the successful beginning under her leadership. Arriving in Tuscaloosa from Atlanta in 1946, Van Duzor served the club during its first fifteen years.

There are many stories about Van Duzor's managerial style. One in particular concerned her devotion to the rule of being on time. One evening, Mildred Warner, president of Gulf States Paper Corporation and donor of the landmark building where the club was located to the University, reserved a table for a dinner party. When she and her guests arrived late, Van Duzor told her the club was closed. With her usual good humor, Warner took her guests to a restaurant across the street. There were others who suffered the same fate, but there was no denying that dining at the University Club was a true gastronomical treat—and worth obeying the rules.

Early members of the club recall other stories about Van Duzor's concern not only with serving the best food but in creating ambience. It was she who nurtured the trees on the lawn and supervised the planting of flowers and shrubbery. Her devotion to beauty led her to extend her talents for organization—some would call it browbeating—to the planting of trees throughout downtown Tuscaloosa, reminiscent of an era when huge oak trees lined what was then Broad Street (now University Boulevard). Van Duzor felt that a beautiful downtown enhanced the lovely antebellum home that faced the city's business district. The planting became known as the "Van Duzor trees" as an homage to the person the *Tuscaloosa News* called "spunky and persistent."

She also lent her talents to Christ Episcopal Church where, as a staunch member, she provided recipes and frequently supervised church meals. Ray Pradat, former rector of Christ Episcopal Church, recalls his nerves during the first sermon at the church. After the service, he was honored with a luncheon planned by Van Duzor. Under great pressure to make a good impression, Pradat was appalled when she said after the luncheon, "Parson, my food would have tasted much better had it been blessed."

Blessed or not, her tempting cuisine attracted many diners to the University Club who requested her recipes. In 1962, she wrote a cookbook, providing authentic flavors in easy-to-follow instructions. These recipes were served on a daily basis at the club, where the cooks were carefully monitored by her and reprimanded if they dared change a pinch of salt.

And now, by popular demand, the club herewith presents the second printing of *Fascinating Foods from the Deep South* exactly as in the original with the addition of a page translating what used to be called No. 2, 3, 4, or 303 cans into ounces. We predict the book will find a favored spot in your recipe library.

Happy cooking in the tradition of the Old South, y'all.

Camille Maxwell Elebash

Fascinating Foods from the Deep South

CHAPTER I

BEVERAGES

KAPPA PUNCH

HOT FRUIT TODDY

HOT RUSSIAN TEA

MRS. RAINER'S PUNCH FOR 100

PUNCH FOR 30 (TEA BASE)

HOT SPICED TOMATO JUICE

PUNCH FOR 100 WITH SHERBET

CHAPTER I

BEVERAGES

Recipes

KAPPA PUNCH (MOCK CHAMPAGNE)

1 large bottle catawba grape juice
2 bottles 7-Up

Pour over large cake of ice.

HOT FRUIT TODDY

(serves 40)

1 qt. orange juice
2 c. lemon juice
1 46-oz. can pineapple juice
½ gal. cider or half cider
 and half cranberry juice

Boil together 5 minutes:
1 c. sugar
2 c. water
1 t. whole cloves
1 T. candied ginger

Strain and mix with fruit juice. Heat in double boiler. Any combination of fruit juices will make fruit toddies when heated.

HOT RUSSIAN TEA

(serves about 60)

1½ gal. boiling water
¼ lb. green tea
3 tea bags (orange pekoe)

Steep these ingredients 5 minutes.

1 T. whole allspice
2 T. whole cloves
1 qt. water

Boil together 5 minutes and strain.

Add:
spices to hot tea
3 c. sugar
1 qt. orange juice
 (1 doz. oranges)
1 c. lemon juice
grated rind of 2 oranges
grated rind of 1 lemon

Heat over hot water—taste. Serve for afternoon or evening reception during the winter.

MRS. RAINER'S PUNCH FOR 100

5½ c. lemon juice (4 doz. lemons)

Boil 5 minutes all lemon rinds in 5 qts. water.

Add:
10 c. sugar
5 qts. cold water
the lemon juice

Cool. All juice equals 11½ qts. liquid. To each 1 qt. of the above add 3 cold Coca Colas. Pour over block ice.

PUNCH FOR 30

3 T. green tea
1 qt. boiling water

Mix, steep 5 minutes, strain, cool.

Add:
1 lb. sugar (stir until dissolved)
1 pt. ice water
juice 8 lemons
grated rind 2 lemons
1 46-oz. can pineapple juice
1/3 46-oz. can grapefruit juice
1 qt. ginger-ale

Fill punch bowl and *then* add ice.

HOT SPICED TOMATO JUICE
(serves 20)

2 46-oz. cans tomato juice, heated

Boil together 5 minutes and strain:

1 large bay leaf
3 t. whole allspice
1/2 c. water

Add:
1 dash tabasco
3 t. salt
3 t. sugar
1 T. Lea & Perrins
1/4 c. lemon juice

Mix all the above ingredients and keep hot in double boiler or over hot water. A substitute for soup; this may be served in punch cups.

PUNCH FOR 100 (WITH SHERBET)

1/4 lb. orange pekoe tea
1 gal. boiling water

Mix and steep 5 minutes, strain and cool.

Add:
1 gal. cold water
2 46-oz. cans pineapple juice
2 46-oz. cans grapefruit juice
1/2 gal. any mixed fruit juice,
3 qts. ginger-ale

Chill thoroughly. When ready to serve fill punch bowl with about 1/3 of the above. Add about 1/2 gal. sherbet and 1 qt. ginger-ale to each 1/3 of the above mixture. Do not add sugar to the above as the sherbet will supply enough.

CHAPTER II

BREADS

BAKING POWDER:

BISCUITS
- Cut
- Drop
  - Peanut Butter
  - Pineapple

CORN BREAD
- Muffins or Sticks
- Spoon Bread
- Egg Bread

GRIDDLE CAKES
- Bread Crumb Cakes
- Orange Suzettes

QUICK LOAF BREADS
- Nut
- Orange-fruit Nut
- Raisin

MUFFINS
- Apple Spice
- Bran
- Plain

SCONES (DATE)

YEAST:

DINNER ROLLS

ORANGE ROLLS

CINNAMON ROLLS

SWEDISH LIMPL

SWEDISH TEA RING

REFRIGERATOR ROLLS

MISCELLANEOUS:

ORANGE TOAST

SUNDAY TOAST FOR SUPPER

TOASTED ROLLS FOR LUNCHEON

CHAPTER II

BREADS

Recipes

Baking Powder Breads

CUT BISCUITS

2 c. sifted flour (all purpose)
3 level t. baking powder
½ t. salt
6 level T. shortening
½ c. milk (approx.)

Sift together: flour, salt, and baking powder. Using 2 knives together, cut shortening into flour mixture. Add milk slowly until all ingredients are in a rather moist ball. Using floured board or waxed paper, place dough in center and sift over it a small amount of flour. With both hands toss it lightly until smooth. Roll out ¼ inch thick and cut into biscuits and place on shallow pans. For variety use fancy cutters: jello molds or cookie cutters. Preheat oven to 450°. Bake about 15-20 minutes at 450° or until nicely brown.

DROP BISCUITS

Use same measurements as for cut biscuits, adding about ⅓ cup milk. Use dessert or tablespoon to pick up a rounded spoonful—push off with a spatula or a knife. Place on greased shallow pans. Bake 15-20 minutes, or until brown, at 450°.

PEANUT BUTTER DROP BISCUITS

Use basic biscuit recipe. Add 4 level T. peanut butter to the dry mixture and cut in shortening. Drop by tablespoonfuls on greased shallow pans or cookie sheet. These will brown more quickly than plain drop biscuits. Bake at 400°.

PINEAPPLE DROP BISCUITS

Use basic biscuit recipe. Add to dry ingredients: ¼ t. soda, ½ c. sugar. Spoon enough crushed pinapple with juice from can into dry ingredients to make consistency for drop biscuits. Drop by tablespoonfuls into greased cookie sheet. Bake at 350° until brown.

CORN BREAD (MUFFINS OR STICKS)

Oil or grease muffin or stick pans, place in oven just long enough to heat. Add batter quickly.

2 c. corn meal
½ c. flour
1 t. salt
3 t. baking powder
3 T. melted shortening
2 beaten eggs
2 c. milk

Sift all dry ingredients together, add the remaining. Beat only to mix together. Preheat oven to 350° and bake.

SPOON BREAD

1¼ c. sifted meal
2 c. water
2 c. milk
2 T. melted butter
1½ t. salt
2 t. baking powder
2 egg yolks, beaten
2 egg whites, beaten

Mix water and meal. Cook over low heat until thick, stirring constantly. Add milk, egg yolks, butter, salt. When smooth fold in beaten egg whites and, last, the baking powder. Pour immediately into greased 2 qt. baking pan. Bake at 350° for 45 minutes or until brown.

EGG BREAD

This is corn bread cooked in a baking pan and cut in squares. *Use basic corn bread recipe* increasing liquid by ½ c. and adding 1 additional beaten egg. Use shallow pan about 7 x 11 inches. Bake at 350°. Bread should not be thick.

BREAD CRUMB GRIDDLE CAKES

Mix:
1 c. sifted dry bread crumbs
1 c. flour
½ t. salt
4 t. baking powder
2 T. brown sugar

Add:
1 well beaten egg
½ c. water
1 c. milk
4 T. melted oleo

Beat and bake on ungreased hot griddle. When full of bubbles, turn and cook the other side. Serve hot with maple syrup. To test griddle for proper heat: Drop ½ t. cold water on hot griddle, if drop stays together and dances on griddle, heat is right for cakes. If too hot, drops will disintegrate. Adjust heat to medium after reaching correct temperature.

ORANGE SUZETTES

(makes 24 small)

2 c. flour
½ c. powdered sugar
1 t. salt
1 t. baking powder
2 c. milk
2 t. grated orange rind
3 eggs beaten well
3 T. melted shortening

Mix well. Beat until smooth. Bake on ungreased griddle. Place in warm bowl and add sauce to each layer. Keep covered. Serve hot. To test griddle, heat about 5 minutes and then drop ½ t. water on griddle. If too hot, water will separate into several drops. If drops stay together, griddle is correct heat.

ORANGE SAUCE

½ stick butter
1 c. powdered sugar
4 t. grated orange rind
1½ c. orange juice

Cream butter and sugar until fluffy. Add orange juice. Heat over hot water in a double boiler.

Quick Loaf Breads

All quick loaf bread should be cooked slowly, cooled on a wire rack, and stored at least 1 day before using. If weather is quite warm, the bread may be wrapped in foil and stored in refrigerator for longer than overnight. *Bread too fresh cannot be cut in thin even slices.* For delicious sandwiches, spread with soft butter or cream cheese.

NUT BREAD

1 egg, beaten
1¾ c. milk
1 c. sugar
2 t. salt
4 c. sifted flour
4 level t. baking powder
2 c. nuts, slightly chopped

Sift together all dry ingredients. Add nuts, egg and milk. Mix well. Pour into greased bread pan. *Let rise 15 minutes* after placing in pans. Makes 2 loaves, 8 x 4 x 3. Bake at 300° for 45 minutes to 1 hour. Turn out on wire rack to cool.

ORANGE-FRUIT NUT BREAD

2½ c. sifted flour
2 t. baking powder
1 t. soda
1 T. salt
1 c. sugar
1 c. nuts (chopped)
1 c. fruits chopped (raisins, crystallized citron, pineapple)
1 T. grated orange rind
2 beaten eggs
1 c. milk
1 c. orange juice
½ stick oleo or butter (melted)

Sift dry ingredients together, add fruits, nuts, orange rind. Combine egg, milk, orange juice. Add flour mixture and melted shortening. Turn into pans which have been greased, paper lined and greased again. Makes 2 loaves, 8 x 4 x 3. Bake at 350° for 50-60 minutes.

RAISIN BREAD

Sift together:
2½ c. whole wheat flour
4 c. white flour
2 T. baking powder
2 T. salt
1½ c. sugar

Add:
3 c. milk
2 eggs, well beaten
4 c. raisins, floured

Pour into 3 greased bread pans and let stand 15 minutes. Bake at 350° for 45 minutes.

PLAIN MUFFINS

½ stick butter (¼ cup)
¼ c. sugar
½ t. salt
2 eggs, beaten
2 c. flour (sifted)
3 t. baking powder
1½ c. milk

Cream *soft* butter and sugar. Add eggs—beat well. Measure and sift together dry ingredients. Add alternately with milk to the butter and sugar mixture. *Do not overbeat or muffins will have tunnels in them.* Spoon batter into hot greased muffin tins. Makes 14 muffins. Bake on rack at 350° for 30 minutes.

For surprise muffins: Before baking drop ½ t. of preserves or jelly on the top of each muffin.

APPLE SPICE MUFFINS

Use plain muffin recipe. Peel 3 apples and cut into eighths or thin wedges. When muffin pans are filled press 3 wedges down into muffin batter, sprinkle sparingly with cinnamon and sugar. Bake at 300° for 25 minutes.

BRAN MUFFINS

1 c. Kellogg's All Bran
1¼ c. milk
1c. sifted flour
3 t. baking powder
½ t. salt
1 egg beaten
4 T. sugar
2 T. melted shortening
½ c. raisins

Mix bran and milk. While sifting together the dry ingredients, add raisins to dry mixture. Combine all ingredients, fill hot greased muffin pans ½ full. Makes 12 muffins. Bake at 350° about 30 minutes or until brown.

DATE SCONES
(makes 18 scones)

2 c. flour
4 t. baking powder
1/4 c. sugar
1/2 t. salt
3 T. butter

Add:
1 1/2 c. chopped dates
1 egg, beaten
1/2 c. milk

Mix into soft dough. Roll out and cut into 2 x 3 inch rectangles 1/4 inch thick. Spread with soft butter and sprinkle with cinnamon. Cut into triangles. Bake at 350° about 20 minutes or until brown.

Yeast Breads

DINNER ROLLS

1 pkg. dry yeast dissolved 10 minutes in 1 c. warm water
3/4 c. shortening
1 c. warm mashed potato
3/4 c. sugar
4 eggs, beaten

Stir all together and let rise 2 1/2 hours or until bubbly.

Add:
2 t. salt
4 c. flour (sifted), enough to make a soft dough

Knead well, place in greased bowl; when risen, make into rolls. Let them double in size. Bake at 350° for 20-25 minutes.

REFRIGERATOR ROLLS

1 pkg. dry yeast
1/4 c. luke warm water
3/4 c. evaporated milk
1/2 c. boiling water
2 eggs, beaten
1/4 c. sugar
1 t. salt
1/4 c. melted shortening
4 1/2 c. sifted flour (approx.)

Soak dry yeast in lukewarm water for 10 minutes. Mix evaporated milk and boiling water. Cool to lukewarm. Combine all ingredients, knead on floured board until smooth. (Do not work in additional flour.) Place in greased bowl, cover with waxed paper. When double in size, knead again, return to bowl, cover well and place in refrigerator until needed. *To use*: Pull off necessary amount, make into balls and flatten or roll out dough and cut. Brush with oleo and turn over for Parker House rolls. Brush the tops with oleo. These must rise until double in size. Bake at 350° for 20 minutes.

ORANGE ROLLS
(makes about 30)

Use basic refrigerator roll recipe with the following: grate rind of 2 oranges, add 1 1/2 c. white sugar. Mix well. Roll out dough to 1/4 in. thickness in a rectangle. Spread with soft oleo.

Sprinkle with orange sugar mixture. Cut dough in half. lengthwise. Roll up as for jelly roll, then cut rolls about ½ inch thick. Place cut side down on greased shallow pan. Let rise until double in size. Bake at 325° or until brown. Mix ½ c. orange junce with 1/2 lb. confectioners sugar. Spread over top of rolls. Serve at once.

CINNAMON ROLLS

Use basic refrigerator roll recipe. Roll out dough into a rectangular piece. Spread with soft oleo. Cover generously with brown sugar. Sprinkle with ground cinnamon. Sprinkle with seedless raisins. Roll up, holding roll firmly in both hands. Cut in ½ inch slices. Place cut side down on greased cookie sheet, leaving about ¼ inch between rolls. Place in warm place. Let rise until double in size. Bake at 350° until light brown (about 15 minutes).

SWEDISH LIMPL
(makes about 24 rolls)

½ c. water
½ c. brown sugar
½ stick oleo
1 t. carraway seed
1 t. anise seed

Boil all together for 3 minutes. Add 1½ c. milk to the above to make a luke warm mixture.

Add:
2 pkgs. yeast (let stand 10 minutes)
2 t. salt
2 egg yolks or 1 whole egg
1 qt. whole wheat flour
Mix well

Add enough white flour to make a soft dough (that leaves the side of the mixer). Let rise until double, work down and make into rolls, and let rise again until double. Bake at 350° until brown.

SWEDISH TEA RING

Use basic refrigerator roll recipe. To 1 qt. of roll dough add: grated rind of 1 lemon, 2 T. sugar, 1 egg or 2 egg yolks. Place in mixer and knead well. Roll to ¼ inch thickness. Spread with soft oleo and brown sugar. Cut in two rectangular pieces. Sprinkle with chopped nuts, citron, currant, white raisins, and candied orange rind (about 2 T. of each.) Roll up as for a jelly roll. Place roll on greased cookie sheet, making a circle. Cut with scissors from outer edge of circle *almost* to inner edges. With tips of fingers turn over each wedge of dough. Let rise 3 hours or until double in size. Bake on rack about 30 minutes at 325°. When brown, remove from sheet to large platter. Spread with icing made from: 1½ c. confectioner sugar, ½ c. water, ½ t. salt, 1 t. vanilla. Serve warm.

Miscellaneous

ORANGE TOAST
(for 12 slices of bread)

½ c. orange juice
1 c. sugar
Grated rind of two oranges
4 T. soft butter

Mix butter and sugar. Add juice and rind. Spread on hot toast and run under flame to melt the sugar.

SUNDAY TOAST

Trim crusts off desired amount of whole wheat bread.

Mix:
⅓ c. brown sugar
1 t. cinnamon
2 T. seeded and chopped raisins
2 T. soft butter

Spread paste on bread and bake in hot oven at 450° until edges are brown. Cut into strips. Delicious to serve with hot tea.

TOASTED ROLLS FOR LUNCHEON

Split day old rolls and dip in undiluted evaporated milk. Sprinkle generously with Parmesan Cheese and bake in oven 15 to 20 minutes at 350°.

CHAPTER III

CAKES & CAKE FROSTINGS

CAKES:

ANGEL CAKE
BEST WHITE FRUIT CAKE
BANANA LAYER CAKE
CARAMEL PARTY CAKE
DEVIL'S FOOD CAKE
DEVIL'S FOOD CAKE DE LUXE
ELEANORA'S WHITE CAKE
BLACK AND WHITE LAYER CAKE
GOLD CAKE
JAPANESE SPICE CAKE
LADY BALTIMORE (SEE FROSTINGS)
PINEAPPLE CRUNCH CAKE
SOUR CREAM CAKE

CAKE FROSTINGS AND FILLINGS:

CHOCOLATE ICING
DE LUXE CHOCOLATE CAKE FILLING
FRUIT FILLING
FOOL-PROOF WHITE ICING
LEMON FILLING
QUICK CARAMEL FROSTING
SEA FOAM FROSTING

CHAPTER III

CAKES AND CAKE FROSTINGS

Cakes

ANGEL FOOD
(makes one cake)

1 c. cake flour
  sifted four times
1½ c. sugar
  sifted with flour once
1¼ c. egg whites
½ t. salt
1¼ t. cream of tartar
1 t. vanilla
¼ t. almond extract

Method using electric mixer: Beat egg whites on high until foamy only—*stop*. Add salt and cream of tartar, beat until whites are in points *only*. Add sugar and beat 2 seconds—*stop*. Add flour, beat on low for 1 second—*stop*. Beat on high 2 seconds—*stop*. Mixture should be smooth. Add flavoring by hand. Pour into ungreased tube cake pan. Bake at 375° for 30 minutes. Invert cake in pan immediately on removing from oven. When cold, run spatula around cake and remove from pan. This cake will be very tender and delicious if these directions are followed.

BEST WHITE FRUIT CAKE

1 lb. butter
1½ lbs. sugar
1½ lbs. flour
2 t. salt
18 eggs
1 lb. citron
2¼ lbs. crystallized cherries
2¼ lbs. crystallized pineapple
1½ lbs. pecans
1½ lbs. almonds
1 c. milk
2 level t. baking powder

Cut cherries, almonds, pecans in half, other fruits in large pieces. Mix lightly with the flour and baking powder. Cream butter and sugar; add eggs, unbeaten, one at the time. Add the fruit mixture. Use four bread pans or 2 tube pans, greased and lined with paper. Bake in bread pans at 275° for 2 hours; tube pans 1½ hours. Some crystallized lemon and orange peel may be used in place of some pineapple and cherries. For flavor and good keeping, a pint of sherry is needed to pour over the cakes when cool.

BANANA CAKE
(makes 2 layers)

1¼ c. sugar
1 stick oleo or butter (soft)
1 t. soda
1 t. vanilla
2 eggs
2 c. sifted flour
¼ c. sour milk
1 c. mashed bananas
1 c. nuts

Place sugar, oleo, eggs, banana, nuts in mixer and beat 2 minutes. Add remaining ingredients. Beat *only* long enough to mix. Place in 2 greased layer cake pans. Bake at 350° about 25 minutes. Put together with foolproof white icing (see icings).

BLACK AND WHITE LAYER CAKE

Use Eleanora's White Cake recipe (below). Spoon half the batter into 1 layer cake pan. To the other half of the batter add 2 squares melted cooking chocolate and 1/3 teaspoon soda, dissolved in 1 teaspoon water. Fill second cake pan with this. Bake at 350 about 20 minutes. Use foolproof white iceing for between layers, and on top and sides. Melt 1/2 package of dot chocolate and dribble over sides and top of cake.

CARAMEL PARTY CAKE

(makes 2 layers)

1½ c. milk, scalded
1 c. sugar
3 c. sifted cake flour
4 t. baking powder
¾ t. salt
¾ c. shortening
1 c. sugar
4 eggs

Heat milk in double boiler. Dissolve 1 c. sugar in heavy frying pan. As soon as melted, pour *slowly* into hot milk. Cool and measure. Add more milk if there is not 1¾ c. of liquid.

Cream shortening and the last 1 c. of sugar. Add eggs, beat well. Add flour and liquid alternately. Bake at 375° for 25 minutes. Cover with Sea Foam frosting (see frostings).

DEVILS FOOD CAKE

(makes 2 layers)

½ cake Baker's chocolate
1 c. milk
½ c. sugar

Cook together until thick. Stir constantly. Remove from fire and add 2 t. vanilla and set aside to cool.

½ c. oleo
1 c. sugar
¾ c. milk
2 eggs or 4 egg yolks
2 c. flour
1 t. salt
2 t. baking soda
3 T. boiling water

Cream oleo and sugar, add 1 egg at the time, and add milk; dissolve soda in boiling water, mix all together, and add flour. When smooth, add chocolate mixture. Bake in 2 greased layer cake pans in moderate oven of 350° for 25 minutes.

Frosting: 2 c. sugar, ½ c. water. Cook until it spins a thread and pour over 4 beaten egg whites. Beat well and add 1 t. vanilla. Spread over cake.

DEVIL'S FOOD CAKE DE LUXE

Use recipe for devil's food cake and use De Luxe chocolate filling with foolproof white icing for the top and sides of the cake (see "Cake Frostings and Fillings").

ELEANORA'S WHITE CAKE
(makes 2 layers)

Cream together:
1/2 stick oleo
1/2 stick butter
3/4 c. sugar

Sift together:
1 T. baking powder
1/2 t. salt
2 c. flour

3 egg whites
1/4 c. sugar
1/4 t. almond extract
3/4 c. milk

To the butter mixture add one-half flour mixture and one-half the milk. When smooth, add remaining flour and milk. Do not overbeat. To beaten egg whites add 1/4 c. sugar, fold into batter, add flavoring. Spoon batter into 2 greased 9-inch layer cake pans. Bake at 350° for 20 minutes, or until cake springs back when touched lightly with finger.

GOLD CAKE
(makes 2 layers)

1 1/4 c. sugar
1 1/2 sticks butter
3/4 c. egg yolks
3/4 c. milk
2 1/2 c. sifted flour

2 1/2 t. baking powder
1/2 t. salt
1/2 t. vanilla
1/4 t. almond extract

Sift together all dry ingredients 3 times. Beat together well the first 4 items. Fold in dry ingredients and flavoring. Place in 2 greased 9-inch layer cake pans. Bake at 375° for about 20 minutes, or until the moment when the cake leaves the edge of the pan. Use any desired frosting.

JAPANESE SPICE CAKE

Use Gold Cake recipe and divide batter into 2 parts. To the first part add: 1/2 c. dark raisins. To the second part add: 1 T. sesame seeds, toasted; 1/2 t. cinnamon; 1/4 t. cloves; 1/4 t. nutmeg. Heat in skillet: 1/2 c. chopped pecans, 1 T. oleo. Stir until brown. Use Sea Foam frosting to cover each layer. Over raisin layer, add pecans. Over spice layer, dust with coconut. Cover sides with Sea Foam frosting also.

SOUR CREAM CAKE
(makes 2 layers)

1 1/4 c. sugar
1/2 c. egg yolks
1/2 stick of soft butter
Beat well together

Sift together:
1/2 t. salt
2 1/2 c. sifted flour
1/2 t. soda
1/2 t. baking powder

Add: 1 1/4 c. heavy sour cream, 1 t. vanilla

Combine all ingredients. Bake in greased layer cake pans about 25 minutes at 375°. Cover with chocolate or quick caramel frosting or any desired frosting.

PINEAPPLE CRUNCH CAKE

(serves 24)

Use pan about 10 x 15 inches or 2 layer cake pans. Use sour cream cake recipe. Place half batter in pan. Cover with 1½ c. drained crushed pinapple. Cover with remaining cake batter.

Top with:

1½ c. cocoanut
1 c. brown sugar
1 c. rice crispies
1 c. chopped nuts
⅔ c. melted butter or oleo

Mix well and sprinkle over cake. Bake at 350° for about 20 minutes. Cut in squares, serve with whipped cream.

Cake Frostings and Fillings

CHOCOLATE ICING

(for a 2-layer cake)

¾ stick oleo
3 sq. Bakers chocolate, melted
1¼ pkg. XXXX sugar
¼ t. salt
1 t. vanilla

Mix all together and add enough evaporated milk to make the right consistency to spread on the *cool* cake.

DE LUXE CHOCOLATE CAKE FILLING

(for a 2-layer cake)

This should be made the day before it is to be used.

1 c. sugar
¼ c. flour
¼ t. salt
3 egg yolks
2 c. scalded milk
2½ sq. Bakers Bitter Chocolate
1 t. vanilla
1 c. chopped nuts (to be added after filling is cooled)

Mix sugar, flour, salt, egg yolks; gradually pour in the scalded milk, stirring constantly. Add chocolate and cook in double boiler for 15 minutes. Stir constantly. Use between layers, cover outsides with white icing.

FRUIT FILLING
(for a 2-layer cake)

¾ c. evaporated milk
¼ c. water
½ c. sugar
¼ c. dates, chopped
¼ c. figs, chopped
¼ c. raisins, chopped
½ c. nuts, chopped
¼ t. grated lemon rind
¼ t. salt
1 t. vanilla

Mix all ingredients except nuts and vanilla. Cook in double boiler until thick. Remove from heat; add nuts and vanilla. This is to be used between the layers of cake. Cake will remain moist for several days with the above filling. Cover outside with any desired frosting.

FOOL-PROOF WHITE ICING
(for a 2-layer cake)

1½ c. white sugar
½ c. water
3 egg whites, beaten stiff
For flavoring: 1 t. vanilla or ½ t. grated orange or lemon rind

Cook sugar and water until syrup immediately spins a thread from a spoon dipped in syrup. Pour onto egg whites. Beat until glossy and thick. Spread on cake.

LADY BALTIMORE ANGEL CAKE FILLING

Use recipe for Fool-Proof White icing. Divide in two parts to one part add:

1 c. choppe nuts
½ c. each white raisins
Chopped chrystallized pineapple, citron, cherries
¼ c. chopped chrystallized orange and lemon rind.

Prepare cake by Angel Food Cake recipe. Split cake crosswise. Cover bottom layer with fruit filling. Add nuts, add top layer, and cover entire cake with remaining white icing.

LEMON FILLING
(for a 2-layer cake)

2 t. oleo
1 c. sugar
3 egg yolks
⅓ c. lemon juice
¼ t. salt
2 T. grated lemon rind
3 T. flour

Mix sugar and flour. Add lemon juice, rind, eggs, and salt. Melt oleo in sauce pan. Add the above mixture. Cook over low heat until thick and filling comes to a boil. *Stir constantly*. This burns easily. This is delicious for a white cake covered with white icing.

QUICK CARAMEL FROSTING
(for a 2-layer cake)

1 stick butter, 1 c. packed brown sugar. Cook 2 minutes, stir constantly. Add ¼ c. milk and bring to a boil, let cool slightly. Add: 2 c. sifted confectioners sugar, 1 t. vanilla. Beat until smooth. Ice cake while icing is warm.

SEA FOAM FROSTING
(for a 2-layer cake)

2 c. brown sugar
4 egg whites
½ c. water
1 c. chopped nuts
1 t. vanilla

Boil sugar and water until syrup spins a thread *immediately* when dipped up with a spoon. Beat egg whites until quite stiff. Pour syrup onto egg whites, beating constantly. Add vanilla. When smooth, apply to cake layers, then add chopped nuts over top.

CHAPTER IV

CHEESE DISHES

CHEESE BALL

CHEESE FONDUE

CHEESE PIE

CHEESE RAMEKINS

CHEESE SOUFFLE

MARY'S CHEESE STRAWS

PIMENTO CHEESE SQUARES

SALLIE'S CHEESE WAFERS FOR TEA

WELSH RABBIT

CHAPTER IV

CHEESE DISHES

Recipes

CHEESE BALL

½ lb. roquefort cheese
4 small pkgs. of Philadelphia cream cheese
1 jar Borden's "Vera Sharp" cheese
1 pkg. Shefford's Snappy cheese
½ c. finely chopped nuts
½ c. finely chopped parsley
1 T. Lea & Perrins
1 garlic button, grated fine
1 t. red pepper or tabasco

Mix until creamy; make into 1 large ball or 2 small ones. Roll in ½ c. chopped nuts and ½ c. chopped parsley. Serve with crackers for buffet supper or for afternoon tea.

CHEESE FONDUE
(serves 6)

2 c. day old bread cubes or toast
½ lb. grated cheddar cheese
3 eggs, separated
1 c. evaporated milk
½ c. water
1 t. salt
1 t. mustard

Mix bread, water, milk; heat until mixture is smooth, stirring constantly. Add grated cheese, seasonings and egg yolks. Fold in beaten egg whites. Fill greased baking dish ¾ full. Set in pan of water. Bake at 350° for 1 hour or until knife inserted comes out clean.

CHEESE PIE

1 c. grated cheese
1 c. bread crumbs (white)
1 c. milk
½ t. salt
2 eggs, beaten slightly

Mix well and pour into greased pan for baking. Bake 20 minutes at 350°. This is a good substitute for macaroni and cheese.

CHEESE RAMEKINS

1 c. bread crumbs
1 c. milk

Cook together until smooth.

Add:
6 T. grated cheese
2 T. melted butter
½ t. mustard

Place over heat for 1 minute and stir. Remove from heat and add:

2 egg yolks, beaten slightly
2 egg whites, beaten stiff
½ t. salt
2 dashes tabasco

Fill buttered ramekins, bake 15 minutes at 350°. Serve *hot.*

CHEESE SOUFFLE
(serves 6)

Make white sauce:

3 T. oleo
4 T. flour
1½ c. milk
1 t. salt

¾ lb. chopped cheese
4 egg yolks, beaten

4 egg whites, beaten

Add cheese to white sauce on low heat. Stir until melted. Add egg yolks and then fold in stiffly beaten egg whites. Bake at 350° for 30-40 minutes. Bake in buttered glass dish. Caution: Do not hurry souffle by increasing temperature of oven.

MARY'S CHEESE STRAWS

¾ lb. grated cheese
3 c. flour, sifted
¼ lb. butter
1 t. salt
⅛ t. pepper or 3 dashes tabasco

Mix all ingredients by hand. Work until soft enough to put through cookie press. Bake at 300° until light brown.

PIMENTO CHEESE SQUARES

½ lb. pimento cheese
⅔ c. oleo or butter
about 60, 1-inch squares of bread

Work the cheese and butter together until soft. Spread bread with medium thin layers of the cheese and butter mixture on all sides but one. Arrange on cookie sheets. Bake at 375° about 15 or 20 minutes. Serve *instantly.*

SALLIE'S CHEESE WAFERS FOR TEA

1 stick butter
1 lb. N.Y. cheese, grated
1 c. flour
½ t. salt
¼ t. red pepper or tabasco

Mix all ingredients together into a dough, make into long rolls about size of a silver dollar. Refrigerate overnight. Slice very thin, place a nut in center. Bake at 250° until brown.

WELSH RABBIT

1 c. flour, 1 c. oleo (2 sticks). Mix until it bubbles. Add 3 qts. milk (can be half water), 1 T. salt, 1 T. Lea & Perrins, 3 dashes tabasco. Let the above come to a boil. 4 c. grated cheese. Add to the above mixture after it boils. Do not allow to boil after cheese is added. Serve on melba toast.

CHAPTER V

COOKIES

AFTERNOON TEA DAINTIES

BUTTER FINGERS

CHEWY CHOCOLATE SQUARES OR BROWNIES

CRESCENTS

CHOCOLATE COCONUT DROP COOKIES

MARY ANN'S COCONUT COOKIES

DATE BARS

DROP COOKIES

MERINGUE SHELLS OR KISSES

MARGUERITES

PECAN SQUARES

PETER PANS

SCOTCH SHORTBREAD

SPRITZ

CHAPTER V

COOKIES

Recipes

AFTERNOON TEA DAINTIES

2 pkgs. cream cheese (3 oz.)
1 stick butter and
  1 stick oleo
2 c. flour
½ t. salt
¾ c. nuts, chopped fine
guava jelly

Cream cheese, oleo, and butter; add flour, salt. Chill in refrigerator several hours, roll thin on floured board. Spread with jelly, sprinkle with nuts. Cut in 4 strips. Roll up like jelly roll and cut in ½ inch slices. Bake on greased sheets for 10 minutes at 350°.

BUTTER FINGERS

1 c. butter
5 T. powdered sugar
2 c. flour
2 c. nuts, broken
1 t. vanilla

Work butter, sugar, and flour together in bowl. Add vanilla and nuts. Form into fingers. Bake in slow oven at 300° until brown and crisp. Roll in powdered sugar.

CHEWY CHOCOLATE SQUARES OR BROWNIES

½ lb. oleo
2 lbs. sugar (4 c.)
1¾ c. flour
1 t. salt
1 8-oz. cake Bakers
  Chocolate (melted)
8 eggs, beaten
1 T. vanilla
½ lb. chopped nuts

Cream oleo and sugar. Add beaten eggs, melted chocolate, and all other ingredients. Bake at 350° until firm to the touch *Caution*: Do not overbake.

CRESCENTS
(about 3½ doz.)

1 stick butter
1 c. nuts, cut fine
4 T. powdered sugar
2 c. sifted flour
¼ t. vanilla and ¼ t. salt

Mix well, roll out, and cut in crescents. Bake at 250° for about 1 hour. Roll in powdered sugar.

CHOCOLATE COCONUT DROP COOKIES
(makes about 2 doz.)

3 sq. chocolate, melted
1 can condensed milk
1 8-oz. pkg. coconut

Mix all together. Drop on greased cookie sheet. Bake 15 minutes at 300°. *Caution*: Do not overbake.

MARY ANN'S COCONUT COOKIES

First part:
1½ c. flour
¾ c. butter
½ c. sugar

Mix together well and pat onto greased baking pan. Bake at 325° until edges are slightly brown.

Second part:
1 c. coconut
1 c. nuts
2 c. brown sugar
3 eggs, beaten separately

Mix these together, fold in beaten egg whites last. Pour onto partly baked crust. Bake 10 minutes at 400° and 30 minutes more at 350°.

DATE BARS
(2 doz. 4-inch bars)

6 eggs, beaten separately
2 c. sugar
4 c. dates, chopped
2 c. pastry flour
2 t. baking powder
1 c. chopped nuts
1 t. salt

To beaten egg yolks add sugar, beat well, add dates, nuts, and dry ingredients. Fold in egg whites which have been beaten stiff. Pour into greased shallow pans, spread evenly. Bake at 375° for 1 hour. Cut in squares, roll in confectioners sugar.

DROP COOKIES
(makes about 3 doz.)

¾ c. powdered sugar
½ c. butter (1 stick)
1 T. ice water
2 egg yolks
½ t. salt
½ t. vanilla
1 c. flour

Drop by the teaspoonful on buttered sheet. Put nut on top and bake at 400°. Leave space between cookies.

MERINGUE SHELLS OR KISSES
(8 shells or 25 kisses)

1 c. sugar
½ c. water
2 egg whites, beaten stiff
½ t. vanilla

Cook sugar and water over brisk heat until it spins a thread when dropped from a spoon. Pour onto egg whites; add vanilla. Beat until glossy. Drop by teaspoonfuls onto a buttered cookie sheet or use pastry bag and form meringue shells. Bake at 200° until very light brown.

MARGUERITES

To the above recipe add ½ c. of each: nuts, chopped; raisins, chopped; crystallized fruits (mixed). Drop onto small salty crackers. Bake at 200° until light brown.

PECAN SQUARES
(makes 49 squares)

Beat 4 eggs until light; add 1 lb. brown sugar. Cook over hot water for 2 minutes. Remove from stove. Sift together: 1½ c. flour, ½ t. salt, 1½ t. baking powder. Combine with first mixture. Add: 1 t. vanilla, 1½ c. chopped pecans. When well mixed, spread ½ inch thick on greased, floured pans. Bake 20 minutes at 350° Cut in squares while warm. *Optional*: When cool, may be covered with Quick Caramel Frosting (see page 22).

PETER PANS
(makes about 4½ doz.)

½ c. white sugar
½ c. brown sugar
1 egg
½ c. butter (1 stick)
4 rounded T. flour
1 c. chopped nuts

Drop by ¼ t. onto buttered sheet. Leave 2-inch spaces between cookies. Bake at 350°. When done, remove immediately from pan. If cookies become too crisp, return to oven long enough to warm and soften to remove from pan.

SCOTCH SHORTBREAD
(makes about 8 doz.)

1¼ lbs. flour
1 lb. oleo
6 ozs. brown sugar
2 t. vanilla
nuts

Mix all of the above ingredients, except the nuts. Make into balls about the size of the end of your thumb. Place half a nut in the inside of each ball. Bake at 375° for 25 minutes. Cool. Roll in powdered sugar.

SPRITZ

1½ c. sugar
2 eggs
2 c. (1 lb.) shortening (half butter)
4 c. flour, before sifting
½ t. salt
1 t. almond flavoring

This makes a stiff dough. Use a cookie press for shaping the cookies on the cookie sheet. Bake at 450° until brown. Keep uncooked dough cold while baking cookies.

CHAPTER VI

DESSERTS

CHOCOLATE:

Chocolate Crumb Pudding
Chocolate Fudge Pudding
Chocolate Roll
Chocolate Souffle
Cousin Cora's Chocolate Ice Box Pudding
Fudge Pie
Sallie's Chocolate Ice Box Dessert

NON-CHOCOLATE:

Some non-pastry desserts are called pie because they appear in the wedge shape of a pie. Such desserts are listed here.

Almond Macaroon Pudding
Angel Charlotte
Apple Crisp
Apricot Bavarian Cream
Butterscotch Pudding
Caramel Baked Custards
Charlotte Russe
Date Nut Angel Pudding
Date Ice Box Roll
Flower Garden Cake
Date Graham Cracker Meringue
Glorified Pudding
Heavenly Pie
Lemon Crunch Dessert
Orange Cream Shortcake
Macaroon Pie
Jessie's Peach Krinkle
Peach Melba de Bouffant
Pineapple Ice-Box Dessert
Bethel's Shortcakes: Peach, Strawberry
Syllabub
Tipsy Pudding—Trifle
Upsidedown Date Pudding

CHAPTER VI

DESSERTS

Recipes

Chocolate

CHOCOLATE CRUMB PUDDING
(serves 8)

In top of double boiler melt:

1 square of bitter chocolate
Add:
½ stick oleo
½ c. milk
¾ c. sugar
4 beaten egg yolks

Cook until thickened, then add:

2 c. soft bread crumbs
1 c. sliced almonds
½ t. salt

Fold in 4 egg whites beaten stiff. Cover and steam in double boiler 25 minutes. Serve hot or cold with cream or custard with grated orange rind.

CHOCOLATE FUDGE PUDDING
(serves 6)

⅓ stick oleo
½ c. sugar
1 t. vanilla
½ sq. bitter chocolate, melted

Mix these ingredients together. Add to the first mixture:

¾ c. flour
1 t. baking powder
⅓ t. salt
6 T. milk
½ c. chopped nuts

Pour into greased pan. Prepare topping mixture:

½ c. brown sugar (packed)
½ c. white sugar
6 T. cocoa
⅓ t. salt

Mix well and sprinkle over cake mixture. *Carefully* pour 1¼ c. boiling water over mixture in pan. *Do not stir.* Bake 1 hour at 350°. This will separate into 2 layers with crust on top and fudge on bottom. Serve crust side down with whipped cream.

CHOCOLATE ROLL
(serves 8)

Beat together:

4 egg yolks
½ c. granulated sugar
4 T. Baker's unsweetened cocoa
½ t. salt
1 t. vanilla

Fold in 4 egg whites beaten stiff. Pour into shallow greased pan. Bake 20 minutes at 300°. Cover wax paper or foil with sifted powdered sugar. Turn out chocolate roll on paper to cool.

Whip:
1 c. heavy cream
½ c. sugar
1 t. vanilla

Cover roll with cream. Roll as for jelly roll and slice. Refrigerate not more than 4 hours.

CHOCOLATE SOUFFLE
(serves 8)

3 egg yolks, beaten
1 c. sugar
½ c. cocoa
2½ T. flour
½ stick oleo
½ c. hot milk
½ t. salt
3 egg whites, beaten stiff

Cook in double boiler until thick. Remove from heat. Beat with egg beater. Add 1 t. vanilla. Fold in egg whites, beaten stiff. Pour into greased pan, set in pan of hot water. Bake at 350° for 45 minutes or until firm. Serve with whipped cream.

COUSIN CORA'S CHOCOLATE ICE BOX PUDDING

4 T. butter
1⅓ c. powdered sugar
4 egg yolks

Beat all together until light. Add:

½ t. salt
2 squares melted chocolate
1 c. chopped nuts
1 t. vanilla

Fold in 4 egg whites beaten stiff. Split 12 lady fingers and line spring-form pan. Add chocolate mixture. Refrigerate 12 hours. Serve with whipped cream. Note: Sponge cake cut in thin strips may be used in place of the lady fingers.

FUDGE PIE
(makes 1 pan)

2 squares bitter chocolate
1 stick oleo
2 eggs, separated
1 c. sugar
¼ c. flour
1 t. vanilla
⅓ t. salt
¾ c. chopped nuts

Melt chocolate and oleo in top of double boiler. Add flour and egg yolks. Beat egg whites until stiff, add sugar and fold into chocolate mixture. Add chopped nuts. Pour into greased pie pan. Bake at 325° about 25 minutes or until *just* firm. *Do not overcook.*

SALLIE'S CHOCOLATE ICE BOX DESSERT

½ c. nuts, chopped
2 T. sugar
¼ lb. vanilla wafers

Crush vanilla wafers and mix with sugar and nuts. Mix and cook in double boiler until thick:

2 egg yolks
6 T. sugar
¼ c. cocoa
2 T. water

Dissolve ½ T. plain gelatin in 2 T. cold water, add to hot custard. Cool slightly and fold in:

4 egg whites, beaten stiff
1 c. heavy cream, whipped
¼ t. salt
1 t. vanilla

Line pan with ½ cookie crumbs. Add chocolate mixture and cover with remaining crumbs. Chill overnight. Serve with whipped cream.

NON-CHOCOLATE

ALMOND MACAROON PUDDING
(serves 24)

2 T. plain gelatin soaked in 1 c. milk

Custard:
1 pt. milk
3 egg yolks
½ c. sugar

Cook in a double boiler until custard coats the spoon. *Do not allow water underneath to boil.* Add soaked gelatin. Chill until it begins to set. Add:

3 egg whites, beaten stiff
1 c. cream, beaten stiff
2 doz. almond macaroons, broken in pieces
1 t. vanilla
1½ t. almond extract
½ t. salt

Sprinkle top with slivered almonds. Refrigerate at least 2 hours. Serve with whipped cream.

ANGEL CHARLOTTE
(serves 8)

1 T. plain gelatin
3 T. cold water
Soak 5 minutes—dissolve over hot water.

Add:
½ c. sugar
¼ t. bitter almond extract
⅓ t. salt

Cool *slightly*. Whip 2 c. cream. Add gelatin mixture. Chop ⅓ c. marachino cherries and ⅓ c. pecans. Sprinkle pan with the chopped cherries and pecans. Add the charlotte. Sprinkle top with nuts and cherries. Refrigerate at least 1 hour.

APPLE CRISP
(serves 8)

6 apples, peeled and sliced thin
¾ c. sugar
1 t. cinnamon
juice 1 lemon
¼ c. water
½ t. salt

Mix all together and place in *greased* baking dish.

Topping:
½ c. sugar
⅔ stick oleo
1 c. flour
½ t. salt

Mix all together until crumbly. Spread over apple mixture. Bake at 350° until apples are tender. Serve with whipped cream.

APRICOT BAVARIAN CREAM
(serves 6)

1 T. plain gelatin
½ c. apricot juice
½ c. sugar
1 T. lemon juice
1 #2 can apricots (drained)
1⅓ c. cream, whipped
¼ t. salt

Soak gelatin in apricot juice 5 minutes. Dissolve over hot water. Press apricots through a sieve. Combine all ingredients except cream. When mixture begins to set, fold in whipped cream.

BUTTERSCOTCH PUDDING

1 c. brown sugar
2 T. butter
2 c. hot milk
2 T. powdered sugar
1 t. vanilla
1-inch thick slice stale bread
2 egg yolks
2 egg whites, beaten
¼ t. salt
juice of ½ lemon

Melt brown sugar and butter over direct heat. Cook until brown *only*. Do not burn. Slowly add hot milk to sugar mixture. Simmer until sugar is dissolved. While the sugar is simmering, soak bread in cold water until soft. Press all water from it. Crumble bread and add to sugar mixture. Also, add egg yolks, salt, vanilla. Pour into buttered baking dish. Set in pan of water and bake for 45 minutes at 350°. To beaten egg whites add powdered sugar and lemon juice. Cover pudding with meringue. Brown lightly in oven. Serve warm or cold. To test pudding: Insert knife; if it comes out clean, pudding is done.

CARAMEL BAKED CUSTARD
(serves 6)

½ c. sugar
3 eggs
2 c. milk
½ t. salt
1 t. vanilla

Brown half of the sugar in a skillet; add ¼ c. water and cook until a thick syrup. Place 1 T. in each custard cup. Mix all remaining ingredients and *carefully* fill custard cups. Set cups in pan with water half way up sides of cups. Bake at 300° until firm, about 1 hour. To test, insert knife in custard. If knife comes out clean, custard is done. To serve: invert cups over sauce dish and slip out custard.

CHARLOTTE RUSSE
(serves 6)

Cook in double boiler until it coats the spoon:

- 1 pt. milk
- 2 egg yolks, beaten
- 1 c. sugar
- ½ t. salt

Soak 2 T. plain gelatin in ¼ c. cold water for 5 minutes. Add to hot custard. Set in pan of cracked ice. When custard begins to set, fold in 1 c. cream, whipped, 2 egg whites, beaten stiff and 1 t. vanilla. Line mold or dessert dishes with lady fingers. Add charlotte. Serve with whipped cream and cherry on top.

DATE NUT ANGEL PUDDING
(serves 6)

- 2 eggs, separated
- 1 c. powdered sugar
- 1 T. flour
- 1 t. baking powder
- ½ t. salt
- 1 c. broken nuts
- 1 c. chopped dates

Beat egg yolks with sugar until *very* light. Add dates, nuts, salt, flour, baking powder. Fold in beaten egg whites. Pour into greased baking pan. Set in pan of hot water. Bake 30 minutes at 300°

DATE ICE BOX ROLL
(serves 6)

- 2 c. corn flakes
- 2 c. bran flakes
- ¾ c. milk
- 1 c. dates (cut in small pieces)
- ¼ c. sherry
- ¼ lb. powdered sugar
- 1 c. marshmallows (cut in small pieces)
- 1 c. chopped nuts

Roll flakes until very fine. Put aside ½ c. crumbs. Combine all other ingredients. Shape into roll. Roll in reserved flakes. Wrap in wax paper or foil. Store overnight in refrigerator. Slice, serve with whipped cream. This dessert can be kept for a week or more.

FLOWER GARDEN CAKE
(serves 14)

- 1 round A&P angel cake, broken into pieces
- 1 T. plain gelatin
- ¾ c. cold water
- *Soak gelatin in water 5 minutes.*
- 6 egg yolks
- ¾ c. sugar
- ¾ c. lemon juice
- 2 t. grated lemon rind

Make custard in double boiler. Remove from heat when it coats the spoon. Add gelatin. Beat 6 egg whites and add ¾ c. sugar. Fold into the custard. Fold in cake. Pour into greased tube pan or spring form pan. Refrigerate at least 6 hours. Unmold, cover generously with sweetened whipped cream.

DATE GRAHAM CRACKER MERINGUE

(serves 6)

2 egg whites	¼ c. nuts, chopped
½ c. sugar	⅓ t. salt
¾ c. graham cracker crumbs	½ t. vanilla
⅓ c. dates, chopped	

Mix cracker crumbs, dates, nuts, salt. Beat egg whites until quite stiff. Add sugar and vanilla. Fold in first mixture. Pour onto greased cookie sheet. Bake at 325° for 25 minutes. Serve with whipped cream.

GLORIFIED PUDDING

1 pkg. zwieback, rolled into crumbs. Reserve 1 c. crumbs. To remaining crumbs. add:

1 stick melted butter	½ c. sugar

Spread on pudding pan, bake in slow oven until hard. Make custard of:

3 c .milk	2 T. cornstarch
4 egg yolks	1 T. vanilla
½ c. sugar	

Cook in double boiler 10 minutes, stirring constantly. When cool, pour over the crust. Cover with meringue made of 4 beaten egg whites and 8 T. sugar. Dust with reserved crumbs. Brown in oven. Serve cold.

HEAVENLY PIE

(makes 3 pies)

8 egg whites	3 c. sugar
½ t. cream of tartar	6 T. shredded coconut

Beat egg whites until stiff but not dry. Add sugar, cream of tartar and beat until stiff. Grease pie pans well. Cover bottom and sides with meringue ½ inch thick. Sprinkle rim with coconut. Bake 1 hour at 275°. Cool.

In top of double boiler place:

8 beaten egg yolks	2 T. lemon rind
1 c. sugar	½ t. salt
6 T. lemon juice	

Cook until thick. Cool. Whip 3 c. heavy cream. Fold into the lemon mixture. Pour into meringue crusts. Must refrigerate at least 12 hours. Top with whipped cream.

LEMON CRUNCH DESSERT
(makes 1 pie)

Crunch:
Cream together:
1 stick soft oleo
1 c. brown sugar

Add:
1 c. crushed wheat flakes
½ c. chopped pecans
½ c. coconut
1 c. flour
½ t. salt

Mix all together. Reserve 1¼ c. for top. Grease pie pan and line bottom and sides with crunch mixture. Fill with lemon mixture: ¾ c. sugar, 2 T. flour, ¼ t. salt, 1 c. water added slowly. Cook over direct heat 3 minutes. Gradually pour onto 2 beaten eggs. Cook in double boiler 5 minutes. Add ⅓ c. lemon juice, 1 t. grated lemon rind. Pour into crunch-lined pan; cover with crunch mixture. Bake at 350° for 40 minutes of until brown. Chill. Serve with whipped cream.

ORANGE CREAM SHORTCAKE
(makes 1 cake)

1 c. flour
1 t. baking powder
½ t. salt
4 eggs, unbeaten
½ c. sugar
½ t. vanilla
2 T. hot water

Place eggs and sugar in bowl over hot water until a little warmer than the hand. Beat in electric mixer for 10 minutes. Add remaining ingredients. Pour into 1 greased paper-lined layer cake pan. Bake at 350° for 15 minutes.

Filling:
3 c. milk
4 T. flour
1 t. salt
¾ c. sugar
2 eggs
grated rind of 1 orange

Scald milk in double boiler. Pour onto sugar and flour mixture. Cook in double boiler 15 minutes. Stir constantly. Pour onto beaten eggs.

Return to double boiler, cook 5 minutes. Split cake. Spread filling over lower half. Cover with orange segments, then cover with other half of cake. Top with powdered sugar. Serve with or without whipped cream.

SALLIE'S MACAROON PIE
(makes 1 pie)

9 small square Premium soda crackers, crushed fine
3 egg whites, beaten until frothy
1 c. sugar added gradually to egg whites.

Fold in cracker crumbs, 1 c. chopped nuts, 2 t. almond extract. Melt 1 T. oleo in pie pan. Pour in mixture. Bake at 300° about 20 minutes.

JESSIE'S PEACH KRINKLE
(serves 5 or 6)

1 c. biscuit mix. Milk enough to make rolled out biscuit. Roll out and cut into biscuits. Dip biscuits into small amount of melted oleo, then in sugar and cinnamon. Overlap biscuits in well-greased pudding pan. Drain #2 can peach halves. Dip peaches in lemon juice, then in brown sugar. Insert peach halves between biscuits and around the edges. Sprinkle with chopped nuts. Bake at 425° for 25 minutes. Serve with cream, plain or whipped.

PEACH MELBA DE BOUFFANT
(serves 1)

Slice of angel cake. 1 large peach half on cake slice. 1 scoop vanilla ice cream in peach half. Red Raspberry jam (beaten to make a sauce) poured over all. Top with whipped cream and a cherry. Serve with salted nuts.

PINEAPPLE ICE BOX DESSERT
(serves 10)

Mix:
½ lb. marshmallows, cut in pieces
1 pt. crushed pineapple (drained)

1 pt. cream, whipped
½ c. sugar
1 t. vanilla
About ¼ lb. vanilla wafers, rolled into crumbs.

Sprinkle bottom of pan with cookie crumbs. Cover with all of pineapple mixture. Cover top with crumbs. Cover lightly with whipped cream. Refrigerate at least 2 hours.

BETHEL'S SHORTCAKE
(serves 6)

2 c. flour
¾ t. salt
3 t. baking powder
1 T. sugar
1 stick oleo or ½ c. other shortening
1 c. milk

Sift together all dry ingredients. Cut in shortening. Add the milk. This must be a very soft dough. Lightly flour board or wax paper. Toss the very soft dough and cut into squares or rounds ¼ inch thick. Bake at 450° until brown. Use while warm if possible. Mashed and sugared peaches or strawberries can be placed between the split shortcake with more on top. Serve with whipped cream. Some people like the shortcake split and buttered while warm.

SYLLABUB FOR A PARTY
(serves 36)

1 qt. heavy cream, whipped. Beat in 3 c. sugar. Add 1 pt. sherry and 1½ qts. cereal cream. Immediately fill punch cups and refrigerate. This will separate with a thick layer on top. This is as it should be. Serve with pound cake or fruit cake.

TIPSY PUDDING
(serves about 6)

Slice stale butter cake and place over bottom of shallow pudding pan. Sprinkle generously with sherry and cover with custard. Set in refrigerator until ready to serve. Top with whipped cream.

Trifle:

Over cake with sherry, spoon raspberry jam; add custard on top.

Custard:

2 c. milk
2 T. flour
½ t. salt
½ c. sugar
2 eggs
½ t. vanilla

Scald milk in double boiler. Pour onto mixed flour and sugar. Cook 15 minutes in double boiler. Stir constantly. Pour onto beaten eggs. Return to double boiler for 5 minutes. Cool. Add vanilla.

UPSIDEDOWN DATE PUDDING
(serves 6)

Combine, cook and cool:
½ c. cut dates
½ c. boiling water

Mix together:
¼ c. white sugar
¼ c. brown sugar
1 t. grated orange rind
1 egg
1 T. melted oleo

Sift together:
¾ c. flour
½ t. soda
¼ t. baking powder
½ t. salt
½ c. chopped nuts

Combine all of the above and pour into a baking pan. Carefully pour over pudding: ¾ c. brown sugar, 1 T. oleo, ¾ c. boiling water. Bake at 375° for 40 minutes. Serve with whipped cream.

CHAPTER VII

EGGS

EGGS CONCORDIA

GOLDEN ROD EGGS

DEVILED EGGS

PUFFY OMELET

CHAPTER VII

EGGS

Recipes

EGGS CONCORDIA
(serves 8)

2 T. oleo
4 T. chopped celery
4 T. chopped green pepper

Cook together 5 minutes. Add: 1½ T. flour and let it bubble

Add:
1½ c. milk
1 #2 can peas (drained
1 4-oz. can mushrooms with juice
2 T. chopped pimento
1 t. salt

Last, add 5 hard boiled eggs, cut in quarters. Just before serving add 1 c. grated cheese, ½ t. Lea & Perrins, and 1 dash of tabasco sauce. Can be used for a chafing dish. Will not *run* on a plate.

GOLDENROD EGGS
(serves 4)

Medium white sauce is the base: 2 T. oleo or butter, 2 T. flour, ½ t. salt. Place in sauce pan and allow to bubble 2 minutes. Add 1½ c. milk. Stir constantly and allow to boil 2 minutes. Hard boil 4 eggs. Separate the yolks from the whites. Chop egg whites and add to the white sauce. Pour over melba or very dry toast. Press egg yolks through a sieve, covering toast. Serve at once.

DEVILED EGGS
(makes 1 dozen)

Place eggs in cold water over medium heat. When they come to a boil, boil 10 minutes. Drain and immediately cover with cold water. Cut in half. Separate yolks from the whites. Mash yolks and add: 1 t. salt, ½ t. French mustard, ½ t. sugar, 1 T. oleo, ¼ t. pepper, 2 T. vinegar, enough water to make a smooth consistency. Fill whites, press tops with a fork.

PUFFY OMELET
(fall-proof — serves 2)

Separate 4 eggs. Beat 3 egg yolks until light with 3 T. water. Add ½ t. salt. Beat 4 egg whites until they will not slip out of the bowl when tipped to one side. In iron skillet melt 2 T. bacon fat or oleo. Allow skillet to heat but not smoke. Fold beaten whites into yolks, using an up-and-down stroke. Pour into hot skillet. Cook on top of range 2 minutes. Bake in 350° oven for 15 minutes. Remove, crease across the middle. With spatula fold over the omelet. Place on warm platter. There are numerous variations—Examples: Spread ½ omelet with grated cheese; Spread ½ omelet with jelly; Spread ½ omelet with grated ham.

CHAPTER VIII

MEAT COOKERY

HOW WE BAKE A HAM

HOW TO BAKE A LAMB LEG

POT ROAST AT ITS BEST

BAKED HAM CROQUETTES

HAM A LA KING

HAM TIMBALES

CURRIED LAMB

JELLIED LAMB MOLD

WOODSTOCK

PORCUPINES (RICE AND MEAT BALLS)

SALISBURY STEAK

BAKED PORK CHOPS A LA MARJORIE

STUFFED BAKED PORK CHOPS

LIVER CAKES

MARION'S JELLIED MOCK CHICKEN LOAF

UNIVERSITY CLUB SUMMER SPECIAL

CHAPTER VIII

MEAT COOKERY

A few necessary tools will eliminate much guess work from meat cookery and add satisfaction:

1. Meat thermometer	4. Cutting board
2. Sharp cutting knife	5. Meat grinder
3. Sharp boning knife	6. Scales

These are valuable aids in all phases of food preparation.

HOW WE BAKE HAM

First—buy only the top grade of the brand of your preference. Select an uncovered pan large enough for the ham. Preheat oven to 350°. Place ham in pan, place pan in oven. Do not cover. After ham has baked an hour or so, insert meat thermometer into the thickest part of ham. When thermometer registers "Ham Tender," remove ham from oven, remove thermometer. Cut off the dark portion of the fat. Cover ham well with brown sugar. Stick generously with whole cloves. Pour over ham about 1 c. of sweet pickle juice or pineapple juice. Return ham to oven and bake until brown.

Before slicing, stand ham on the larger end and, with the boning knife tight against the bone, cut down to the large end. Place knife on the other side of the bone and repeat. Result—you will have 2 long narrow pieces (like a loaf of bread), free from bone. Slice ham in medium slices and serve with a spoonful of pan gravy over it. The part not used may be wrapped in foil and refrigerated for some time.

HOW TO BAKE A LAMB LEG

Buy only spring lamb. A leg will weigh 6-7 pounds. Have leg bone cut off at the first joint. Wipe meat with damp cloth. Place roast in pan with a rack and tight fitting cover. Insert garlic clove in one end of roast. Over the leg sprinkle 1 T. salt, 2 T. Lea & Perrins and cover with sliced onion.

Preheat oven to 350°. Add 1 c. water to pan and cover. Bake at 350° until meat thermometer reaches LAMB, approximately 3½ to 4 hours. Remove from pan. Skim fat from stock in pan. Proportion for gravy: 1 T. fat; 2 T. flour; to each cup liquid (stock and water).

POT ROAST AT ITS BEST

Various cuts of beef have been used for pot roasts. We prefer the 3 cornered piece of the rump or sirloin tip. Brown beef all over, beginning with the fat surface and using an iron skillet if possible. When browned on all sides remove meat to a pot with a tight-fitting cover. Add 1 c. water to the skillet and pour this brown gravy into the pot. Salt and season. For a 3 lb. roast, use about 1 t. salt and 2 t. Lea & Perrins. Cover tightly and cook on low heat several hours (4-5) until tender. During this time *all water must cook out at least 1 time* and meat must brown further in the drippings. Then add 1 c. water to continue cooking. These extra brownings are necessary to acieve the rich delicious flavor and the brown gravy to be served with each slice.

Recipes

BAKED HAM CROQUETTES
(serves 5)

- ¾ lb cooked ham, ground
- ¾ c. soft bread crumbs
- 1 t. mustard
- 1 T. brown sugar
- ½ t. grated onion
- 2 T. horseradish
- 1 egg, beaten
- ¾ c. milk

Mix all ingredients. Make into cone-shaped croquettes. Dip into beaten egg. Roll in dry bread crumbs. Place on a well greased, shallow pan. Brush with melted butter. Bake at 350° for 30 minutes. Serve with cheese or mushroom sauce. Garnish with sautéed pineapple slices or cinnamon apple slices. Use 2 small croquettes per serving.

HAM A LA KING
(serves 6-8)

In a sauce pan place: 4 T. flour, 4 T. melted oleo. Allow to bubble. Add: 2 c. liquid (juice from 4 oz. can mushrooms and milk); ½ t. Lea & Perrins; 2 T. pimento, chopped; 1 4-oz. can mushrooms; 1 pt. diced ham. *No salt.* Stir until mixture boils 2 minutes. Serve on toast or Holland Rusks.

HAM TIMBALES
(serves 8)

- 2 c. milk
- 1 c. bread crumbs
- 2 c. chopped cooked ham
- 3 T. butter or oleo
- 3 egg yolks, beaten
- 3 egg whites, beaten stiff

Place milk and crumbs in sauce pan over heat. Stir until a smooth paste. Add ham, butter, egg yolks. Fold in egg whites. Fill greased custard cups ⅔ full. Set in pan of hot water, cover cups with wax paper. Bake at 350° until timbales are firm, about 30 minutes. Turn out, serve with cheese or mushroom sauce. Garnish with parsley.

CURRIED LAMB
(serves 8)

Sauté together:	*Add:*
3 T. fat	4 T. flour
1 T. curry powder	2 t. salt
1 small onion, chopped	3 c. liquid (stock or water)

Stir with wire whip to avoid lumps. Add 1 qt. of cooked lamb, cut in small pieces. Cover and simmer 30 minutes on low heat. Serve on steamed rice and if possible—chutney.

JELLIED LAMB MOLD
(serves 8)

Use any lean cut of lamb (neck or shoulder)—3 lbs. lamb; 1 onion (med. large), sliced; 1 T. salt; 1 qt. water. Simmer until tender, discard bone and all fat. Skim fat from broth, reserve. Cut meat in small pieces. Use a pan or mold, about 1 qt. size. Place in bottom 3 or 4 slices of hard boiled egg. Cover with half chopped lamb. Cover with thin layer chopped celery. Add 1 c. small canned peas. Repeat the layers. Boil down liquid to about 3 cups. Season with Lea & Perrins and heat. Dissolve 2 T. gelatin in 1 c. water for 2 minutes. Add to hot stock and spoon over mold. Refrigerate 2 hours. Turn out on chilled serving plate. Garnish with lettuce, sliced tomato and avocado. A meal-in-one for hot days.

WOODSTOCK (in patty shells)
(serves 6)

1 c. medium white sauce (see sauces)	1 c. cooked veal, chopped
2 T. chopped pimento	1 t. salt
1 4-oz. can mushrooms	½ t. Lea & Perrins
2 hard cooked eggs, chopped	1 dash tabasco

Mix all ingredients and serve quite hot in patty shells.

PORCUPINES (rice and meat balls)
(serves 7-8)

	Mix:
2 lbs. ground raw beef	1⅓ c. tomato puree
½ c. uncooked rice, washed and drained	1⅓ c. water
2 t. salt	1 large onion, grated
Mix well and make into 14 or 16 balls.	1 T. Lea & Perrins

Cover meat balls with the liquid mixture and bake at 350° for 1 hour. Serve 2 balls per person.

"OUR" SALISBURY STEAK
(serves 4)

1 lb. sirloin tip beef
1/8 lb. beef fat
1 t. flour
1 egg yolk
2 t. salt

Grind meat and fat twice to make it very fine. Add other ingredients. Mix well by hand. Make into 4-oz. patties. Broil on hot ungreased pan or griddle. Desired results will not be achieved with just *any* meat, or that ground in a market.

BAKED PORK CHOPS A LA MARJORIE
(serves 6)

Brown 1-inch thick pork chops in *very small* amount of fat. Place in baking pan with tight cover. On top of each chop place: 1-inch thick ring of peeled acorn squash; in center, place 3 dried apricots and 2 large dried prunes. Sprinkle with 1 t. salt. Grate rind of 2 oranges. Mix rind and juice and pour over pork chops. Cover and bake at 350° for 1½ hours. Baste several times.

STUFFED BAKED PORK CHOPS
(serves 6)

Have pork chops cut double thick or 1½ inches. Have a pocket made in each chop. Salt chops lightly.

Stuffing:
3 c. cold corn bread
2 c. stale bread (biscuits, rolls, or loaf)
½ c. celery, chopped
¼ c. onion, chopped
1 t. sage, rubbed
½ t. salt
½ t. celery seed

Mix together thoroughly, add about ½ c. boiling water or enough to make stuffing crumbly. With teaspoon, fill pocket in each chop; fasten with tooth pick. Place chops in covered roaster with rack. Pour ½ c. water in pan. Cover and bake at 350° until tender, about 2½ hours. Turn chops once. Serve with pan gravy.

LIVER CAKES
(serves 6)

1 lb. beef or pork liver
1 medium-large onion
6 soda crackers
1 t. salt
3 T. evaporated milk
2 eggs, beaten slightly

Using the medium blade of the food chopper, grind the first 3 items. Add remaining ingredients. Mix well. Mixture will be very soft. Drop by rounded spoonfuls into a skillet containing small amount of bacon fat (3 T.). Brown on both sides. Acceptable for those who do not like the flavor of liver. Delicious served with crisp bacon.

MARION'S JELLIED MOCK CHICKEN LOAF
(serves 10-12)

1 lb. lean veal
1 lb. lean pork
1 large onion, sliced
1 t. salt
3 c. water

Simmer all together until very tender. Remove meat from stock, cool and grind meat. Use medium blade of grinder. Cool stock, skim and boil down to 1 cupful. Soak 2 T. gelatin in ½ c. water. Dissolve in hot stock, cool. Hard boil 3 eggs. Separate yolks and whites, mash each. To the yolks add:

3 T. vinegar
2 t. salt
¼ t. pepper
1 T. sugar
2 T. mustard

Add to ground meat, stir well. Add all other ingredients and 1 c. mayonnaise—taste. Pour into mold, refrigerate 4 hours.

UNIVERSITY CLUB SUMMER SPECIAL
(1 large steamed hen makes 12 servings)

1 slice rye bread (dark with seeds). Spread with a mixture of equal parts of Rouquefort cheese, French's mustard and mayonnaise. Place on top of each other thin slices of: Swiss cheese; Ham; Chicken; ½ inch slice of lettuce. Cover all with 1000 Island dressing (about ½ c.). Garnish with: 2 slices tomato; 1 hard boiled egg, cut into 2 pieces; 2 dill strips or olives.

CHAPTER IX

PIES AND TARTS

PASTRIES AND SHELLS

PIES

Cheesey Apple Pie

Chocolate Chip Almond Pie

Deep Dish Apple Pie

Frozen Fudge Pie

Glazed Strawberry Pie

Plum Glazed Cheese Pie

Pecan Pie

Red Raspberry Cream Pie

Rena Madges' Chess Pie

Roberta's Lemon Ice Box Pie

CHIFFON PIES

Chocolate Chiffon Pie

Margaret's Chocolate Pie

Mary's Lemon Pie

Pirates Lime Chiffon Pie

Rum Chiffon Pie

Peppermint Chiffon Pie

Raspberry or Strawberry Chiffon Pie

TARTS

Blueberry

Butterscotch

Chocolate

Coconut cream

Lemon

Hot Mince

Pineapple

CHAPTER IX

PIES AND TARTS

PASTRIES AND SHELLS

Pie-making will be much easier and more pleasure if you will have on hand in the refrigerator 2 dry mixtures for pie crusts. These mixtures will keep for weeks. Pastry by weight: 1 3/4-lbs. shortening; 3 lbs. flour (all purpose); 2 T. salt; 1 T. baking powder.

For 1 pie shell: 1 cup of pastry mix with *barely* enough ice water to make a very stiff dough. Flour the board and rolling pin lightly and do not add additional flour to pastry. Roll to 1/4-inch thickness.

Graham cracker crust mix: Using the fine blade, grind 1 box of graham crackers. Mix with 2 sticks melted oleo.

Place 1 c. in a pie pan and pat into place on the bottom and around the sides of the pan.

TART SHELLS

Cut pastry for tart shells with a #2½ can. Place on backs of muffin pans. Prick with a fork. Bake at 375° until light brown. Remove from muffin pans, place on cookie sheet and fill.

PIE SHELLS

Roll pastry a little larger than the pie pan. Place pastry on the back of the pie pan. Hold pan in the left hand and with knife in the right hand cut pastry along the edge of the pan. Prick the pastry with a fork. Bake at 375° until light brown. Remove from back of pan, place inside pan and fill.

Recipes

PIES

CHEESEY APPLE PIE

See Pastry for recipe for the crust.

2 c. pastry mix (2 crusts)
1 c. grated cheddar cheese

Mix with ice water and roll out for bottom and top crusts.

Filling for pie:
4-5 large apples, peeled and thinly sliced
1 c. sugar
2 T. flour
½ t. salt
Unless apples are green, add juice of 1 lemon

Mix all ingredients. Fill 9-inch pie pan and cut 4 slits in top crust. Bake at 400° until brown (about 30 minutes).

CHOCOLATE CHIP ALMOND PIE

3 eggs
½ t. salt
1 t. vanilla
1½ c. white Karo Syrup
1½ T. flour
½ c. milk
1 c. slivered or sliced almonds, toasted
1 c. semi-sweet chocolate chips
⅓ c. sugar

Beat eggs slightly. Add all other ingredients, except almonds. Pour into unbaked 9-inch pie shell. Bake at 375° for 30 minutes or until pie sets. Sprinkle almonds over it and bake 15 minutes more. Cool. When ready to serve add whipped cream ruffle around the edge of pie.

DEEP DISH APPLE PIE
(serves 7-8)

Use 2 qt. baking pan. Fill ¾ full of sliced, peeled apples. Add juice of 1 lemon. Mix: ¾ c. sugar; 2 t. flour; ½ t. salt. Sprinkle over the apples. Cut ⅓ stick of butter into slices over apples. Cover with pastry. Make holes on top of pastry. Bake at 350° until brown.

FROZEN FUDGE PIE

⅔ box XXXX sugar
2 eggs
½ t. salt
3 squares Baker's chocolate (melted)
1 c. chopped pecans
1 t. vanilla
1⅓ c. cream, whipped
⅓ box vanilla wafers (about 1 c. crumbs)
2 T. melted oleo

Sift sugar and salt, add eggs, vanilla. Place in mixer, beat 5 minutes until *quite* thick. Add nuts and melted chocolate. Beat 2 minutes. Mixture should be quite stiff. Mix wafer crumbs with melted oleo. Pat into a 9-inch pie pan. Cover with chocolate mixture. Beat cream until stiff, add ½ t. vanilla, 1 drop oil of peppermint, 2 T. sugar. Spread cream over chocolate mixture. Sprinkle with crumbs. Freeze overnight.

GLAZED STRAWBERRY PIE

1 baked 9-inch pie shell
1 qt. large berries, hulled
1 pt. heavy cream, whipped
¼ c. sugar
⅓ c. milk
1 t. vanilla
3 c. cake (buttercake) crumbs, coarse
1 glass red currant jelly melted with 1 T. butter

Fill pie shell with cake crumbs. Mix whipped cream, milk, sugar. Cover crumbs with the cream. Stand berries thick, points up, in cream. Cool melted jelly, spoon over pie. Refrigerate at least 1 hour. Note: This pie can be made *only* during the season for large, fresh berries.

PLUM GLAZED CHEESE PIE

1 lb. plums which have been peeled, seeded
½ c. sugar
⅓ c. water
3 drops red coloring
1 t. cornstarch
2 t. water

Cook plums, sugar, water, coloring, until plums are tender. Mix cornstarch and water. Pour hot mixture onto the cornstarch. Cook 2 minutes. Chill plums and juice.

Bake 9-inch graham cracker crust at 325° for 5 minutes. Cool.

2 small pkgs. cream cheese
⅓ can condensed milk
1 T. and 1 t. lemon juice
1 t. grated rind
½ t. salt
½ t. vanilla
1 c. heavy cream, whipped
2 beaten egg whites

Beat cheese in chilled bowl. Gradually add milk, lemon juice, rind, salt, and vanilla. Fold in beaten egg whites and whipped cream. Pour into crust. Place plums (round side up) over filling. Spoon glaze over all. Place in freezer 2-3 hours. Note: This pie can be made only during the season for fresh prune plums.

PECAN PIE

3 eggs
½ c. brown sugar
2 T. flour
1½ c. dark brown Karo syrup
½ t. cinnamon
½ t. salt
1 t. maple flavoring
½ c. milk
2 T. melted butter or oleo

Line 9-inch pie pan with pastry. Cover with pecans (about 1½ c.). Mix all above ingredients, pour over pecans. Bake at 325° *only* until pie is set.

RED RASPBERRY CREAM PIE

(serves 8)

1 c. heavy cream, whipped
1½ t. plain gelatin
¼ c. cold water
2 egg whites, beaten
¾ c. sugar
1/8 t. salt
1 10-oz. box frozen red raspberries, thawed

Dissolve gelatin in cold water 5 minutes, melt over hot water and cool. Beat egg whites just to peaks. Add sugar, gelatin, salt, and fold in whipped cream. Then fold in raspberries. Pour into baked pie shell (see pastry); refrigerate for 3 hours.

RENA MADGE'S CHESS PIE

4 eggs
1¾ c. sugar
2 t. vanilla
2 t. vinegar
2 t. corn meal
1 stick melted butter or oleo

Beat eggs with a spoon. Add ingredients in order given, beating after each addition. Line 9-inch pie pan with unbaked pastry, pour into pie pan. Bake on bottom rack for 10 minutes at 350°; then at 300° until slightly shaky (about 30 minutes).

ROBERTA'S LEMON ICE BOX PIE

1 graham cracker crust. 4 egg yolks, grated rind of 1 lemon—beat until quite thick. Add juice of 2 lemons, 1 can condensed milk. Beat another 5 minutes. Pour filling into 9-inch crust, cover with meringue: Beat 4 egg whites until they are in peaks, add 8 T. sugar and beat until stiff. Bake at 350° until brown. Refrigerate 2 hours.

CHIFFON PIES

CHOCOLATE CHIFFON PIE
(serves 8)

1½ ozs. unsweetened chocolate
½ c. milk
Soak:
2 t. plain gelatin
2 t. cold water

¾ c. white sugar
½ t. salt
2 t. grated orange rind
1 c. heavy cream, whipped
1 egg white, whipped

Melt chocolate in milk in top of double boiler over hot water. Beat with rotary beater. Add softened gelatin, sugar, salt, and orange rind. Chill until almost set. Whip cream, fold in chocolate mixture and beaten egg white. Pour into a 9-inch baked pie shell and refrigerate 3 hours.

MARGARET'S CHOCOLATE PIE

3 (10c) Hershey Bars with almonds, 18 marshallows (cut), and ½ c. milk—Place these 3 ingredients in double boiler over hot water to melt. When cool, fold in 1 c. cream, whipped, ½ t. salt, 1 t. vanilla. Pour into 9-inch graham cracker crust. Refrigerate at least 3 hours. This may be served with piping of whipped cream.

MARY'S LEMON PIE

½ T. plain gelatin
2 T. cold water
4 egg yolks
½ t. salt
1 c. sugar
grated rind of 1 lemon

juice of 1 lemon
4 egg whites, beaten
1 c. cream, whipped
2 T. sugar

1 baked pastry shell

Soak gelatin in 2 T. cold water 5 minutes. Dissolve over hot water. Mix egg yolks, lemon juice and rind, salt, ½ c. sugar in top of double boiler. Cook until thick, stirring constantly. Add gelatin and cook 1 minute longer. Beat egg whites to peaks, add remaining ½ c. sugar. *Gently* fold hot mixture into egg whites. Pour into a 9-inch baked pastry shell. Cool. Top with cream whipped. A frill of cream adds to the appearance of the pie.

PIRATES LIME PIE

3 eggs, separated; 1 can condensed milk; 1 can limeade concentrate. In a large bowl beat egg yolks until creamy. Add condensed milk and beat until quite thick. Add limeade and a few drops green coloring. Fold in stiffly beaten egg whites. Add 1 t. gelatin soaked in 1 T. water and dissolved over hot water. Turn into a 9-inch baked pie shell. Bake at 300° for 10 minutes.

RUM CHIFFON PIE
OR
EGGNOG PIE

1 baked pie shell
1 c. milk, scalded
2 egg yolks, beaten
2 egg whites, beaten
¾ c. sugar
1 T. plain gelatin soaked in 2 T. water
½ t. salt
1 c. cream, whipped

Mix egg yolks, sugar, and salt. Add scalded milk. Cook in a double boiler until custard coats the spoon. Remove from heat immediately. Add soaked gelatin. Place in a bowl of cracked ice until custard begins to set. Add 3 T. rum and fold in beaten egg whites and whipped cream. Pour into a 9-inch baked pie shell. Refrigerate at least 2 hours. Decorate with whipped cream.

PEPPERMINT CHIFFON PIE

Follow recipe for Rum Chiffon Pie, omitting the rum. To the cooked custard add 2 drops oil of peppermint and enough red coloring for a light pink color (2 or 3 drops). Pour into baked pie shell. Place in refrigerator for 2 hours. To serve, spread pie with whipped cream and cover with grated bitter chocolate.

RASPBERRY OR STRAWBERRY CHIFFON PIE

Dissolve and allow to thicken: ¾ box raspberry or strawberry Jello; 1 c. boiling water; 6 T. sugar. Whip until light and fluffy. Fold into the gelatin mixture: 2 egg whites, beaten stiff; ¾ c. heavy cream, beaten; 1 10-oz. box frozen berries (thawed). Pour into a 9-inch baked pie shell. Chill 2 or 3 hours. Serve with a frill of whipped cream around the edge of the pie.

TARTS

BLUEBERRY TARTS
(about 12)

3 boxes blueberries (frozen, 10 oz. each)
1 c. sugar
3 T. corn starch
2 T. lemon juice
½ c. water

Mix all together. Cook over low heat about 15 minutes. Stir occasionally. Cool and fill baked pastry shells. Serve with whipped cream.

BUTTERSCOTCH TARTS
(about 8)

1 c. brown sugar
3 T oleo

Cook together in sauce pan until sugar is melted.

3 T. white sugar
3 T. flour
3 egg yolks
½ t. salt
1½ c. milk

Mix the above ingredients, eliminate lumps. Add to the melted sugar. Cook over direct heat until thick, stirring constantly. Remove from heat. Add 1 t. vanilla. Fill tart shells. Cover with meringue made with 3 egg whites, 8 T. sugar, and 2 t. lemon juice. Bake at 350° until brown.

CHOCOLATE TARTS
(6-8 tarts)

3 T. cocoa, 3 T. flour, ½ t. salt, ¾ c. sugar—Mix together and add: 1½ c. milk. Stir over low heat until it comes to a hard boil. *Caution*: this burns easily. Pour onto 3 beaten egg yolks. Return to heat for 2 minutes. Add 2 T. butter or oleo and 1 t. vanilla. Cool to lukewarm. Fill cooked pastry shells. Cover with meringue: 3 egg whites beaten with 6 T. sugar. Bake at 350° until brown.

COCONUT CREAM TARTS
(6 tarts)

3 T. sugar, 3 T. flour, ½ t. salt—Mix with 3 T. cold milk. In a double boiler heat 1 c. milk. Pour hot milk slowly into cold flour mixture. Use wire whip to stir and avoid lumps. Return to double boiler, cook 15 minutes, stirring constantly. Beat 2 egg yolks with 3 T. sugar. Pour hot mixture onto egg yolks. Return to double boiler and cook 2 minutes more. Add

2 T. butter. Cool, add ½ t. vanilla and 1½ c. grated fresh coconut. Cover with meringue: 2 beaten egg whites and 4 T. sugar. Sprinkle with coconut. Bake at 375° until brown.

LEMON TARTS

(8 tarts or 1 pie)

Mix all together:	*Add:*
1 c. sugar	1⅓ c. hot water (hot)
⅓ c. flour	3 T. lemon juice
1 t. grated lemon rind	3 egg yolks
½ t. salt	2 T. butter or oleo

Boil all together 3 minutes over direct heat. Stir constantly. Do not allow to scorch. Cool to lukewarm and fill cooked shells. Cover with meringue made with: 3 beaten egg whites, 6 T. sugar, 1/8 t. salt. Bake at 350° until brown.

HOT MINCE TARTS

To 1 can of the *best* rum flavored mincemeat add 1 chopped apple. Place in double boiler to cook apple and heat mincemeat. For serving: Fill tart shells with hot mincemeat and top with hard sauce. See sauces.

PINEAPPLE TARTS

Mix well:	*Add:*
½ c. sugar	1 T. lemon juice
2 T. cornstarch	1 t. grated lemon rind
2 T. flour	1 c. crushed pineapple
½ t. salt	2 t. melted butter or oleo
	¾ c. boiling water

Place all ingredients in a double boiler and cook 15 minutes, stir constantly. When clear looking, pour onto 3 beaten egg yolks. Return to boiler for 3 minutes more. Cool to lukewarm. Fill cooled pastry shells. Cover with meringue: 3 beaten egg whites, 6 T. sugar. Bake at 350° until brown.

CHAPTER X

POULTRY

BROILED CHICKEN
BROILED CHICKEN MARJORIE
TEXAS BARBECUE
RED BARBECUE
SAUTÉED CHICKEN BREASTS
ALMONDINE
BOMBAY SAUCE
SAUCE CHAMPIGNON
CHICKEN BRUNSWICK STEW
CHICKEN CONTINENTAL
CHICKEN DIVAN
CHICKEN HASH
CHICKEN HAWAIIAN
CHICKEN LIVERS WITH PINEAPPLE AND ALMONDS
CREAMED CHICKEN AND MUSHROOMS
OLD FASHIONED CHICKEN PIE
OVEN FRIED CHICKEN—PARMESAN

CHAPTER X

POULTRY

Recipes

BROILED CHICKEN

Best size for broiling is 1½ lbs. Split chickens in half. Sprinkle with salt, refrigerate for several hours. Before broiling, rinse off salt and pat dry with paper towel. With a brush lightly cover both sides with equal parts of melted oleo and bacon fat. Place on a shallow pan, skin side down. Use directions of your range for broiling. Turn chicken. When brown on the boney side and brown on the top side, remove to pan with cover. Use ½ c. hot water to clean off broiling pan and pour this water over chickens. Cover, cook at 350° for 45 min. Result—delicious, tender chicken.

BROILED CHICKEN MARJORIE

(serves 4)

Follow directions for broiled chicken, using 2 chickens. After they are brown on skin side, sprinkle well with paprika. Place in baking pan with ¼ c. water. Cover and bake 45 minutes at 350°. Drain fat from baking pan into sauce pan and add: 1 sliced small onion, 2 T. chopped parsley, 1 T. flour. Sauté 5 minutes. Add: ½ c. cream (heavy whipping), 1 4-oz. can mushrooms with juice, ¼ c. stuffed olives sliced. Allow sauce to boil up and pour over chickens in pan. Cover and bake another 5 minutes. Caution: Do not over-cook after sauce has been added to chicken or sauce will curdle. Serve on toast points, generously spooning sauce over chicken.

TEXAS BARBECUED CHICKEN

Follow directions for Broiled Chicken. After chicken has cooked in covered pan for 30 minutes add Texas Barbecue Sauce and return to oven for 15 to 20 minutes. Sauce for 6 servings:

½ stick oleo melted
½ t. salt
2 T. Lea & Perrins
1 T. sugar
4 T. flour
½ t. chili powder
1 T. dry mustard
¼ c. lemon juice
½ c. vinegar
½ c. hot water
3 dashes tabasco

Mix all ingredients and stir over heat until sauce boils. Pour over chickens.

RED BARBECUED CHICKEN

Follow directions for Broiled Chicken. After chicken has been cooked in covered pan for 30 minutes, add Red Barbecue Sauce and return to oven for 15 to 20 minutes. Sauce for 6 servings:

2 t. mustard	½ c. water
1 T. brown sugar	1 c. catsup
1 t. salt	¼ c. grated onion
¼ c. vinegar	

Simmer all together for 10 minutes.

SAUTÉED CHICKEN BREASTS
(serves 6)

For chicken breast with stuffing, use whole breast weighing about 8 ozs. For chicken breast with a sauce, use half of a large breast weighing about 12 ozs. Breasts purchased already cut need to be wiped off with wet paper towel, salted lightly on both sides, and refrigerated for a few hours. At preparation time, rinse off salt and wipe dry. Melt ½ stick of butter or oleo in a skillet, add chicken breasts and brown slowly on both sides.

CHICKEN BREAST ALMONDINE
(serves 4)

Use medium sized whole breasts. Sauté in skillet with ½ stick butter or oleo. Remove chicken to covered baking pan. To fat in the skillet add: 1 8-oz. can mushrooms (drained), 1 T. grated onion, 2 T. flour, ½ c. slivered almonds. Stir until brown. Add ½ c. mushroom liquid. This should be quite thick. Fill the whole chicken breast, fasten with tooth-picks. Stand up so the filling will not run out. Bake 30 minutes at 350° or until tender. Pour over all ½ c. white wine return to oven for another 15 or 20 minutes. Serve on toast points.

SAUTÉED CHICKEN BREAST—BOMBAY SAUCE

Remove chicken from skillet to covered baking pan. To fat in skillet (about 4 T.), add:

1 t. curry powder	¼ t. nutmeg
1 T. flour	1 t. salt

Stir until smooth and then add:

1½ c. pineapple juice	½ c. raisins
1 T. lemon juice	½ T. sugar
¼ c. coconut	

Pour sauce over the half chicken breasts, cover, bake at 350° until tender (about 30 minutes). Serve on steamed rice.

SAUTÉED CHICKEN BREAST WITH SAUCE CHAMPIGNON
(serves 6)

Remove chicken from skillet to covered baking pan. To fat in skillet (about 4 T.) add 2 8-oz. cans mushrooms, drained, (reserve liquid), 2 T. finely chopped onion. Cook gently 5 minutes. Do not brown. Add: ½ c. heavy cream, mushroom juice, 1 t. salt, ½ c. sherry. Pour sauce over chicken breast. Cover pan, place in oven, cook at 350° for 30 minutes. Serve with steamed rice.

CHICKEN BRUNSWICK STEW
(serves 20)

Disjoint a 5 lb. hen as for frying. In a large pot with a tight cover place: layer of salt pork, cubed; layer of chopped white onion; layer of diced potatoes; layer of corn cut from the cob; layer of butter beans; layer of sliced tomatoes. Add the chicken rolled in flour. Repeat all layers, pork, onion, etc. Add 2 qts. boiling water. Simmer 3 hours. Season with 2 T. salt, 3 T. Lea & Perrins. Cook another hour. Just before serving add 3 T. butter and 3 T. flour mixed with small amount of liquid from the stew. Cook another 5 minutes. Remove chicken bones.

CHICKEN CONTINENTAL
(serves 14-18)

Cook 1 large hen (4-5 lbs., about 6 cups). Separate bones from meat and cut meat into cubes. Grind skin and add to meat.

½ c. flour
½ c. chicken fat or oleo
Cook until bubbly, add:
2 4-oz. cans mushrooms
6 oz. can water chestnuts (sliced)
2 c. chicken stock
¾ t. ground ginger
¼ t. cinnamon
¼ t. nutmeg
1 t. grated lemon rind
¾ c. chopped onion
1½ c. buttermilk

Simmer all together about 20 minutes (taste for salt). Serve on chow mein noodles.

CHICKEN DIVAN
(serves 8)

1 large hen (5-6 lbs.) steamed with 1 c. water under the rack. When tender remove from pan, cool, and slice. Reserve broth. Cook 2 10-oz. boxes frozen broccoli spears, use boiling salted water. Drain. Place cooked broccoli in servings in a large pan. Cover with sliced chicken. Spoon sauce over each portion. Sprinkle thinly with buttered bread crumbs and toasted slivered almonds on top. Bake at 400° for 15 minutes.

Sauce: 1 stick butter or oleo, 8 T. flour, 1 t. salt. Cook together until it bubbles. Slowly add 3 c. milk and broth; stir until smooth. Add 1 8-oz. can mushrooms with juice. When sauce comes to a boil remove from heat and add ¼ c. sherry.

CHICKEN HASH
(serves 12-14)

The usual idea of chicken or turkey hash is that is is made from the "tag ends." Delicious hash may be made with all the flavor and no "tag ends." Take one large hen (4-5 lbs.) scrubbed and salted inside and out and refrigerated overnight. Before cooking, rinse thoroughly. Place in large pot with rack in the bottom and a tight-fitting cover. Add 1 qt. water and simmer (*not* boil) until tender (for about 1½ hrs.) Remove bones from meat and cut meat into cubes, grind up the skin and add the following: 6 end pieces of bread cut in cubes and sautéed until very light brown in 3 T. chicken fat (skimmed from the broth), 1 t. ground sage, 1 t. celery seed, ½ c. grated onion, 1 qt. chicken stock or broth. Simmer 30 minutes.

CHICKEN HAWAIIAN
(serves 6)

3 large chicken breasts (12-14 ozs.) cut into two pieces
1 stick oleo
½ can #2 crushed pineapple
1½ T. chopped crystallized ginger
1 T. soy sauce
1 c. water

Roll chicken lightly in flour; brown in oleo. Pour into covered pan and add other ingredients. Bake 30 to 45 minutes, or until tender.

Serve with almond currant rice: Cook 1½ c. rice with 2 t. salt, until tender when pressed between forefinger and thumb. Place rice in colander or strainer, rinse with hot water, place strainer over pot containing boiling water and steam dry. Just before serving, add: ½ c. currants, ½ stick melted oleo or butter, ½ c. toasted slivered almonds. Stir rice with fork. To serve, place chicken on top of rice, spoon over all any sauce from pan. Note: Salt chicken breasts 1 hour before cooking, rinse off.

CHICKEN LIVERS WITH PINEAPPLE AND ALMONDS
(serves 8)

Sauté together for 10 minutes:
2 lbs. chicken livers
½ stick oleo
Add:
1 #2 can pineapple chunks, drained
1 c. slivered almonds
¼ c. firmly packed brown sugar
¼ c. flour
1 T. salt
1½ c. pineapple juice (from chunks)
6 T. vinegar
1 T. soy sauce

Cook all together 10 minutes. Serve on steamed rice.

CHICKEN TETRAZZINI
(serves 15-20)

Good for buffet supper or church supper. 1 large hen (4-5 lbs. cooked as for chicken hash). Separate bones from meat and cut meat into strips.

Sauce:
¼ c. flour
¼ c. chicken fat
1 small clove garlic, chopped
Cook until bubbly.

Add:
1 c. milk
1½ c. chicken stock
½ t. salt
2 t. Lea and Perrins
2 dashes tabasco

Stir and allow to come to a boil. Cook ¾ lb. spaghetti in boiling salted water. When tender, drain in colander or sieve; rinse with hot water. Combine chicken, sauce, spaghetti, and 3 4-oz. cans mushrooms which have been sautéed in 1 T. chicken fat. Add mushroom juice. Stir until well mixed and add 2 c. Parmesan cheese. Fill chafing dish.

CREAMED CHICKEN AND MUSHROOMS
(serves 8-10)

Steam until tender 1 large hen (5-6 pounds) with 1 c. water under the rack. When cool pull meat from frame, cut meat into medium large pieces, grind skin.

Sauce:

¾ c. chicken fat or melted butter
¾ c. flour

Place in sauce pan over heat until it bubbles. Slowly add

3 c. liquid (using chicken stock, mushroom liquid, evaporated milk)
1 8-oz. can mushrooms, drained
2 t. Lea & Perrins
2 dashes tabasco

Taste for salt. Serve in patty shells or on egg bread squares.

OLD FASHIONED CHICKEN PIE
(serves 10)

1 large hen steamed until tender with 1 c. water under the rack. Pull meat from the frame. Cut into medium large pieces. Grind the fat. Place chicken and fat in pan. Slice 2 hard boiled eggs over it. Pour sauce over all and spoon 3 T. extra chicken fat or melted butter over the top of the sauce. Cover with strips of biscuit dough rolled *very* thin. Bake until brown.

Sauce:

⅓ c. chicken fat or oleo
⅓ c. flour
1 t. salt
2½ c. chicken stock and water

Bring to a boil, spoon over chicken.

OVEN FRIED CHICKEN — PARMESAN

Cut chicken in pieces as to fry, or buy such pieces as breasts and thighs. Salt lightly and refrigerate over night. In morning, rinse salt from chicken. Dry on paper towels. For about 8 pieces of chicken melt ½ lb. oleo. Mix: 1 c. dry bread crumbs (*not* cracker crumbs), ½ c. grated parmesan cheese. Roll chicken in oleo, then in crumbs. Place in a shallow pan. *Do not crowd.* Bake uncovered 1 hour at 350°.

CHAPTER XI

SALADS AND SALAD DRESSINGS

SALADS:

Avocado Dream Salad
Alline's Jellied Fruit Salad
Chicken Salad
Cole Slaw de luxe
Country Salad
Frozen Fruit Salad with Dressing
Crab Salad
Cranberry Salad
Cucumber and Cheese Salad
Hot Potato Salad
Kate's Christmas Salad
Louise's Chicken Aspic
Mustard Beans
Shrimp Salad
Tomato Aspic
Virginia's Molded Chicken Salad
Tossed Salads—Lettuce Roquefort

SALAD DRESSINGS:

French Dressing (also Roquefort)
Mayonnaise
1,000 Island Dressing
Cooked Salad Dressing
Tomato French Dressing

CHAPTER XI

SALADS AND SALAD DRESSINGS

Recipes

Salads

AVOCADO DREAM SALAD
(serves 12)

3 pkgs. lime Jello
1½ c. boiling water
1 #1 flat crushed pineapple (drained)
2 c. pineapple juice
⅛ t. salt
3 T. lemon juice
½ c. mayonnaise
½ c. heavy cream, whipped
1 c. avocado diced

Dissolve jello in 1½ c. boiling water. Add pineapple juice and pineapple. Cool until syrupy. Beat. Fold in mayonnaise, whipped cream, and all other ingredients.

ALLINE'S JELLIED FRUIT SALAD

Drain all juice from the canned fruits to be used in the salad. Royal Anne Cherries or Bing Cherries may be added to any fruit salad. Our basic combination is crushed pineapple, grapefruit sections, peach halves (cut twice). Mandarine oranges may be used in place of grapefruit, etc.

To serve 8:

2 pkgs raspberry Jello
1 c. boiling water

Stir until thoroughly dissolved.

Add:
3 c. fruit juices
1 #303 can grapefruit sections
1 #303 can peaches (cut twice)
1 #1 can crushed pineapple

Refrigerate at least 4 hours.

CHICKEN SALAD
(serves 8)

1 hen, 5-6 lbs.
3 c. chopped celery
1 c. chopped mixed sweet pickle
3 dashes tabasco sauce
3 T. salad oil
2 T. lemon juice
½ t. salt

Salt chicken inside and out and refrigerate overnight. When ready to cook, rinse thoroughly inside and out. Place hen on rack in pot with tight-fitting cover, add ½ c. water. Cover and steam until tender. Cool. Pull meat from bones. Cut white meat in medium sized cubes, dark meat in smaller pieces. Grind skin in medium grinder and add to the chicken. Add the salad oil, lemon juice, and salt. Stir well; refrigerate at least one hour.

Add celery, pickle, tabasco sauce, and enough mayonnaise to bind together. Garnish with capers and serve with sweet peach pickle.

COLE SLAW DELUXE

(serves 10)

2 t. salt
1 t. dry mustard
2 t. celery seed
6 T. sugar
½ c. chopped green pepper
2 T. chopped pimento
1 t. grated onion
⅓ c. salad oil
⅔ c. vinegar
6 c. chopped cabbage

Place all ingredients in a large bowl. Mix well. Cover and chill.

COUNTRY SALAD

(serves 8)

½ lb. cooked smoked ham (about 3 c.)
2 cooked potatoes, diced
4 cooked carrots, diced
½ c. cooked green peas
½ c. cooked lima beans
2 pieces celery, chopped
2 hard boiled eggs, diced
3 T. grated onion
¼ c. India Relish
1 T. horseradish
½ c. mayonnaise
¼ c. vinegar
½ t. salt

Mix all ingredients thoroughly, cover and chill at least an hour before serving. Serve in a lettuce cup with tomato wedges, crackers. A hearty most delicious salad for a complete luncheon.

FROZEN FRUIT SALAD FOR 12

1 #2 can crushed pineapple
1 #2 can sliced pineapple
1 #303 can apricot halves
1 #303 can peach halves
1 #303 can Royal Anne Cherries
¾ c. marachino cherries
¼ lb. marshmallows, cut
1 c. nuts, chopped
½ c. orange juice
¾ c. pineapple juice
1¼ c. sugar
2 T. plain gelatin
1½ c. mayonnaise
1 qt. heavy cream, whipped

Drain all of the fruit. Soak the gelatin in pineapple juice. Add sugar, dissolve over hot water. Add orange juice. Chill until thickened. Add fruits, etc., cut in medium small pieces. Fold in mayonnaise, whipped cream. Pour into shallow pan, freeze over night.

Dressing:

1 c. sugar
½ c. flour
1½ c. pineapple juice
⅓ c. egg yolks (about 4)
½ t. lemon juice
1 t. salt

Mix sugar, flour, pineapple juice. Cook in double boiler 20 minutes. Stir constantly. Pour onto beaten egg yolks. Return to heat for 2 minutes more. Add lemon juice, and salt and chill. To use: Add ⅓ c. whipped cream to the above.

CRAB SALAD

Use only unfrozen crab meat for salad. When crab is frozen much of the moisture seems to disappear, and salad made from frozen crab will be dry and tasteless as compared with the unfrozen crab.

- 1 lb. crab meat (white or mixed with dark)
- 3 hard boiled eggs
- 2 c. chopped celery
- 1 c. chopped dill pickles
- 1 T. horseradish
- Juice 1 lemon
- ½ t. salt
- 3 dashes tabasco

Pick over crab meat to eliminate all shell. Chop the eggs and combine with all other ingredients. Do not add mayonnaise until ready to serve, or salad will be watery. Serve in lettuce cups. Garnish with tomato wedge and lime.

CRANBERRY SALAD
(serves 12)

Cook until tender: 1 qt. or 1 lb. cranberries, 2 c. water—Do not strain. Add 1¾ c. sugar. Cook 5 minutes more. Soak 3 T. plain gelatin in ⅔ c. cold water for 5 minutes. Add to the hot cranberries. Chill until slightly thickened. Add: 1 c. chopped celery, ½ c. chopped nuts, ½ c. orange, chopped, ½ c. crushed pineapple. Mix all together and refrigerate several hours.

CUCUMBER SALAD
(serves 8)

- 1 T. plain gelatin
- 3 T. cold water
- ½ t. salt
- ¾ c. chopped or grated cucumber (1 small)
- 3 T. grated onion
- 2 c. cottage cheese
- 5 oz. cream cheese
- 4 T. mayonnaise
- 4 T. cooked salad dressing
- ½ c. finely chopped celery
- ½ c. nuts, toasted and chopped

Soak gelatin in cold water, dissolve over hot water. Peel cucumber and remove seed. Grate or grind onion and cucumber. Beat cheese together until blended. Add all ingredients and a drop or 2 of green coloring. Fill molds ⅔ full. Serve with cucumber slices which have been chilled in vinegar.

HOT POTATO SALAD

Peel 5 potatoes and boil in salted water. When tender, drain off water, shake potatoes to make dry. Keep hot. Fry until crisp ¼ lb. breakfast bacon, drain on a paper towel. To the fat add:

- ¼ c. vinegar
- ½ t. salt
- 2 t. sugar
- 2 t. mustard
- 1 c. chopped celery
- ½ c. onion, chopped

Leaving potatoes in the pot, with a fork break potatoes in rather large pieces. Pour over them the hot vinegar mixture. Stir well, do not make potatoes mushy. Add crumbled bacon. Keep warm for serving.

KATE'S CHRISTMAS SALAD

(serves 8)

1½ T. plain gelatin
½ c. cold water

Soak together 5 minutes, place over hot water to melt. Add 5 T. sugar. Stir until sugar is melted.

Add:
2 c. water
½ c. fruit juice
4 T. lemon juice
green coloring to make a pretty color

Set in refrigerator until it begins to thicken. Remove from refrigerator and add:

1 #1 can sliced pineapple, cut in pieces
½ c. sliced stuffed olives
½ c. sliced maraschino cherries
⅓ c. slivered almonds

Pour into small molds. Refrigerate several hours.

LOUISE'S CHICKEN ASPIC

2½ T. plain gelatin soaked in 2 c. stock

Add:
3 c. hot stock (chicken or consomme)
3 T. lemon juice
3 dashes tabasco

Allow to set long enough to become syrupy.

Add:
½ small can pimentoes, chopped
½ c. sliced olives
2 c. chopped celery
½ c. nuts, chopped
4 c. cooked chicken (about one medium hen), chopped (not ground)
½ c. sherry

Pour into 15 molds.

MUSTARD BEANS (COLD SALAD)

(serves 8)

Use 1 box French cut beans cooked by directions on package and chilled; or, 3 #2 cans blue lake whole beans.

Mix with:
1 c. mayonnaise
4 T. prepared mustard
6 t. horseradish
2 T. chopped onion
2 T. vinegar
1 t. salt

Chill thoroughly. Serve on lettuce. Garnish with pimento strips.

SHRIMP SALAD

(serves 12)

5 lbs. shrimp
5 hard cooked eggs, chopped
4 c. celery, chopped
1 c. chopped dill pickle
3 dashes tabasco sauce

Place shrimp in kettle of boiling water with 2 t. salt. After shrimp comes to a boil cook 10 minutes. Shuck and devein shrimp. Cut, length-wise, in half. Mix all other ingredients with just enough mayonnaise to bind. Serve at once.

TOMATO ASPIC

(serves 8)

Cook together 10 minutes:

3 T. chopped parsley
2 T. sugar
1 t. whole cloves
3 T. chopped onion
1 c. chopped celery tops
1¼ c. water

Strain and add 3 T. plain gelatin soaked 5 minutes in 1½ c. cold water. Stir until gelatin is dissolved.

Add:
2 t. salt
3 T. vinegar
2½ T. lemon juice
2 c. tomato puree
3 dashes tabasco sauce

Pour into pan and place in refrigerator until aspic begins to thicken, then add: 1 small cucumber, chopped fine, 2 c. chopped celery. Stir well, pour into the molds.

VIRGINIA'S MOLDED CHICKEN SALAD

1 T. plain gelatin
2 T. cold water
½ c. hot water or stock
2 T. vinegar
1 t. salt
2 t. sugar
1½ c. cooked chicken, diced
½ c. celery, chopped
1 T. pimento
⅓ c. mayonnaise
⅓ c. almonds, chopped

Soak gelatin in cold water. Dissolve in hot water. Cool. Combine with other ingredients. Pour into 6 or 8 molds.

TOSSED SALADS

For the best tossed salads, a wooden salad bowl is necessary. This can be rubbed with garlic before the ingredients are placed in the bowl and a smoothness of flavor results when greens and vegetables are mixed. For salad, ingredients should not be finely chopped and may have variety or consist of lettuce only.

LETTUCE ROQUEFORT

(for 6)

1 large head of lettuce, coarsely cut; 4 T. french dressing. Toss well in wooden bowl rubbed with garlic. Sprinkle top with 3 T. Roquefort cheese or Danish blue cheese. Toss once more lightly. Serve at once.

Salad Dressings

FRENCH DRESSING

⅔ qt. salad oil
⅓ qt. vinegar (apple cider vinegar)
2 T. salt
1 T. sugar
1 T. Lea & Perrins
1 clove of garlic (cut in two)

Place all ingredients in a fruit jar and shake until thick. This will keep in refrigerator for a week or two. But *shake* each time it is used.

For Roquefort Dressing: Buy imported Roquefort or *Danish* Blue cheese. With a knife chop cheese until pieces are about the size of a pea. For 1 c. French dressing add 3 T. chopped imported cheese. No other cheese will give the desired result.

MAYONNAISE

1 qt. salad oil
4 T. vinegar
1½ t. salt
3 egg yolks
1½ T. sugar
2 t. Lea & Perrins
1½ T. mustard (French's)

In the bowl of an electric mixer place the egg yolks, salt, and vinegar. Beat at high speed until thick. Reduce speed to low, add oil slowly and all other ingredients. When smooth and thick add 1 T. water. Increase speed for a minute or two.

THOUSAND ISLAND DRESSING

Hard boil 4 eggs, cool and mash.

Add:
1½ c. mayonnaise
1½ c. chili sauce
¼ c. catsup
2 T. Lea & Perrins
2 t. salt
2 T. horseradish
Chopped pickle may be added if you wish

Pour into a jar, cover well. Will keep for several days.

COOKED SALAD DRESSING

2 T. salt
2 T. dry mustard
½ t. tabasco sauce
¾ c. flour
¾ c. sugar
4 eggs, beaten
1 tall can of evaporated milk
1 can water
1½ c. vinegar

Mix all ingredients and cook in double boiler 20 minutes. Stir constantly until quite thick and flour taste has disappeared. Store in a covered jar. Will keep in refrigerator for several weeks.

TOMATO FRENCH DRESSING

1 c. Campbell's tomato soup
¾ c. salad oil
½ c. sugar
1½ t. salt
¾ c. cider vinegar
¼ t. paprika
1 t. mustard
2 T. Lea & Perrins

Mix dry ingredients. Add remaining ingredients, beat (or place in jar and shake until thick). Will keep in refrigerator in a covered jar for a long time.

CHAPTER XII

SAUCES

FOR DESSERTS:

Butterscotch
Chocolate
Orange
Minted Pineapple
Wine
Hard Sauce

FOR MEAT AND VEGETABLES:

Cocktail
Different Sauce for Pork
Sauce Champignon
Sauce Remoulade
Sour Cream
Supreme Sauce
Spanish Omelet Sauce
Raisin Sauce for Ham and Tongue
Tangerine Sauce for Roast Duck
White Sauce
Mock Hollandaise
Barbecue Sauce (Red)
Texas Barbecue Sauce
Bombay Sauce
Tartare Sauce

CHAPTER XII

SAUCES

Recipes

For Desserts

BUTTERSCOTCH SAUCE

4 T. butter
1¼ c. brown sugar (packed)
⅔ c. dark corn syrup

Boil over direct heat until a very soft ball is formed when dropped in cold water. Remove from heat, cool slightly.

Add:
¾ c. evaporated milk
½ t. salt
1 t. vanilla

Stir well, refrigerate covered.

CHOCOLATE SAUCE

(serves 6)

1½ sq. bitter chocolate
2 T. water
½ c. sugar
½ t. salt
1½ T. white corn syrup
½ c. evaporated milk
1 t. vanilla

Melt chocolate over hot water. Add water, sugar, salt, syrup, cook over direct heat until a soft ball is formed when dropped in cold water. Remove from heat. Add milk and vanilla.

ORANGE SAUCE FOR GINGERBREAD

2 c. orange juice
2 T. grated orange rind
1 stick butter
2 c. powdered sugar

Cream butter and sugar, add juice and rind, heat over hot water.

MINTED PINEAPPLE SAUCE FOR ICE CREAM

1 #2 can crushed pineapple
¾ c. sugar
1 c. white corn syrup
2 drops oil of peppermint
3 drops green coloring

Boil all together for 10 minutes.

WINE SAUCE

(For Gingerbread and Puddings)

3 c. powdered sugar
6 egg yolks
6 egg whites
¾ c. wine (sherry)
¼ t. salt

Beat egg yolks until very light. Add half the sugar and beat again. Beat egg whites, add remainder of sugar. Fold together, add ¾ c. wine.

HARD SAUCE

2 sticks butter, 1 lb. confectioners sugar. Beat together until very light. Drop in one whole egg. Beat three minutes. Slowly add ½ c. sherry.

For Meat and Vegetables

COCKTAIL SAUCE

½ c. chili sauce
½ c. catsup
4 T. lemon juice
4 T. horseradish
2 T. Lea & Perrins
2 dashes tabasco sauce
1 t. salt

Mix all ingredients. Serve on crab or shrimp.

DIFFERENT SAUCE FOR PORK

1 c. strained apple sauce
1 c. cream, whipped
1 c. horseradish
1 T. sugar
½ t. salt

Mix all together, serve with pork roast or chops.

SAUCE CHAMPIGNON (FOR CHICKEN)
(serves 10)

2 8-oz. cans mushrooms drained (reserve liquid)
2 T. finely chopped onion

Place in skillet where chicken breasts have been sautéed and cook gently 5 minutes. Do not brown.

Add:
½ c. heavy cream
Mushroom juice
1 t. salt
½ c. sherry

SAUCE REMOULADE (FOR SHRIMP)
(serves 6)

2 c. mayonnaise
½ c. chopped dill pickle
2 T. chopped capers
3 hard cooked eggs, finely chopped
3 T. horseradish
1 T. prepared mustard
1 T. chopped parsley
½ t. salt

SOUR CREAM SAUCE (FOR STEAMED CABBAGE)

2 c. sour cream, whipped until stiff
4 T. horseradish
2 T. onion juice
1 t. salt

Mix gently, serve over wedges of steamed cabbage.

SUPREME SAUCE (FOR BROCCOLI, CAULIFLOWER, ETC.)

1 c. butter
2 T. flour
1 c. lemon juice
1 t. salt
1 small can pimento, chopped

Cook butter and flour until it bubbles, add remaining ingredients. Stir and cook until sauce comes to a boil.

SPANISH OMELET SAUCE

4 T. bacon fat
1 medium onion, chopped
1 medium green pepper, chopped
1 c. celery, chopped

Sauté 3-5 minutes, do not brown.

Add:
1 c. tomato puree
1 8-oz. can mushrooms with juice
1 #2 can green peas, drained
2 T. salt
1 T. Lea & Perrins
3 dashes tabasco

Allow to come to boil. Remove from heat.

RAISIN SAUCE FOR HAM AND TONGUE

Mix:
¼ c. flour
⅓ c. brown sugar
½ t. salt

Add:
1 qt. hot water

After sauce has boiled 2 minutes over direct heat, add 1 c. raisins. Let boil up again, remove from heat. Add 2 T. lemon juice.

TANGERINE SAUCE FOR ROAST DUCK

Drain 1 #2½ can mandarin orange sections. To the orange juice add enough duck broth to make 2 c.

Mix:
3 T. cornstarch
1 t. majoram
1 t. salt
4 T. crystallized ginger chopped
2 6-oz. cans frozen tangerine concentrate

Add orange juice mixture and cook until sauce is thick. Boil 2-3 minutes. Add orange sections. Baste duck with small amounts of sauce last hour of baking. Serve remainder over duck.

WHITE SAUCE (MEDIUM)

½ lb. butter
1 c. flour

Cook over low heat until it bubbles.

Add:
2 qts. hot milk (or half water and half evaporated milk)
2 T. salt

Stir constantly and cook until it has come to a boil. Boil 2 minutes. Do not allow to stick.

Smaller amounts:

2 T. butter	4 T. butter
2 T. flour	4 T. flour
1 c. milk	2 c. milk
½ t. salt	1 t. salt

For a thick white sauce double butter and flour content of medium sauce.

MOCK HOLLANDAISE SAUCE (FOR VEGETABLES)

4 T. flour	2 T. salt
4 T. butter	juice of 2 lemons
1½ c. water	2 beaten egg yolks

Mix flour and butter, stir until it bubbles, add water and salt. Cook until sauce thickens. Pour *onto* beaten egg yolks, add lemon juice. Cook 2 minutes, remove from heat. Sauce can be stored in refrigerator for some time.

BARBECUE SAUCE (RED)

2 t. mustard	½ c. water
1 T. brown sugar	1 c. catsup
1 t. salt	¼ c. grated onion
¼ c. vinegar	

Mix all together and allow to come to a boil. Remove from heat.

TEXAS BARBECUE SAUCE (FOR HALF CHICKEN OR PORK CHOPS)

(serves 6)

2 t. salt	2 T. dry mustard
½ c. melted butter	½ c. lemon juice
4 T. Lea & Perrins	1 c. cider vinegar
2 T. sugar	1 c. hot water
½ c. flour	6 dashes tabasco sauce
1 t. chili powder	

Mix all ingredients, allow to come to a boil, pour over chicken or chops. Cook for 30 minutes.

BOMBAY SAUCE FOR CHICKEN BREAST

(serves 6)

1½ c. pineapple juice	1 t. salt
1 T. lemon juice	¼ c. coconut
1 T. flour	½ c. raisins
1 t. curry powder	½ T. sugar
¼ t. nutmeg	

Place all ingredients in skillet where chicken breasts were sautéed, stir until smooth.

TARTARE SAUCE (FOR FRIED SEA FOODS)

1½ c. mayonnaise	1 T. grated onion
1 t. prepared mustard	3 T. chopped dill pickle
1 T. horseradish	

CHAPTER XIII

SEAFOODS

BALTIMORE CRAB CAKES
CRAB A LA NEWBURG
CRAB FLAKES AU GRATIN
CRAB GUMBO
CRAB NOODLE CASSEROLE
DEVILED CRAB
LOBSTER THERMIDOR
FRIED OYSTERS
MRS. YOUNG'S SCALLOPED OYSTERS
BAKED RED SNAPPER CREOLE
ANNA'S SHRIMP LOUISIANNE
BARBECUED SHRIMP
SHRIMP GUMBO
SHRIMP RAMEKINS

CHAPTER XIII

SEAFOODS

Recipes

BALTIMORE CRAB CAKES

(serves 6)

Sauté together 3 minutes:
- 1 T. oleo or butter
- 1 medium small onion, chopped
- 1 small green pepper, chopped
- 2 T. chopped celery

Add:
- 1 beaten egg
- 1½ c. soft bread crumbs
- 1 lb. crab meat
- ½ t. salt
- ½ t. mustard
- ¼ t. dried thyme
- 2 t. chopped parsley
- 2 T. mayonnaise
- 2 dashes tabasco

Mix all together well. Make into 12 small balls. *Chill at least 1 hour.* Dip in beaten egg plus one T. water. Roll in dry bread crumbs. Fry in deep fat.

CRAB A LA NEWBURG

- ½ c. flour
- 1 stick oleo or butter
- 1 t. salt
- 3 c. milk
- 2 dashes tabasco
- 1 t. Lea & Perrins
- 1/8 t. mace
- 1 lb. crab meat

Cook flour and butter until it bubbles. Add milk slowly. Stir constantly until it comes to a boil. Add all remaining ingredients. Just before serving add ¼ c. sherry. Serve at once on Melba toast.

CRAB FLAKES AU GRATIN

- ½ c. melted oleo
- ½ c. flour
- 1½ t. salt
- 3 c. milk

Mix oleo and flour and let bubble well. Slowly add the milk, stir constantly. Boil two minutes. Add salt. To the white sauce add 1 lb. crab meat, 1 dash tabasco sauce, 1 t. Lea & Perrins' sauce. Mix well. Fill 9 ramekins, leaving space for topping of grated sharp cheese and (last) buttered dry bread crumbs. Bake at 350° until light brown.

CRAB GUMBO

(serves 6-8)

Cut ⅓ lb. breakfast bacon into cubes. Slice 1 c. onion, 2 c. cut okra. Cook together 2 minutes.

Add:
2 c. canned tomatoes, chopped, with juice
1½ c. tomato juice
1 clove of garlic, chopped
1 lemon, thinly sliced
1 bay leaf
1 T. Lea & Perrins
3 dashes of tabasco
1 T. salt
2 c. boiling water

Simmer 1 hour.

Add:
2 T. oleo mixed with 2 T. flour
2 c. or 1 lb. crab meat (free of bone)

Continue to simmer 5 minutes more. Serve in soup bowls with steamed rice ring.

CRAB NOODLE CASSEROLE
(serves 8)

Make a white sauce with 2 T. oleo or butter, 2 T. flour, 1 t. salt—Stir over heat until it bubbles, add 2 c. milk; stir constantly until it boils. Sauté together: 2 T. oleo or butter, 1 green pepper, chopped; ½ c. celery, chopped. Add this to the white sauce. Stir in 1 lb. crab meat and 1 8-oz. can mushrooms, with juice. Boil 1 pkg. noodles and drain. Place noodles in bottom of baking pan, pour crab mixture over them. Top with buttered crumbs. Bake at 350° until brown.

DEVILED CRAB

Sauté together:
3 T. melted oleo
4 T. celery, chopped
4 T. green pepper, chopped

Add:
3 T. flour
2 c. milk
1 lb. crab meat
1 t. salt
1 dash tabasco saue
1 t. Lea & Perrins

Allow to boil for 5 minutes. Fill 7 cockle shells. Top with buttered crumbs. Bake at 400° for 10 minutes, or until brown. Remove at once from oven or the crab will dry out.

LOBSTER THERMIDOR
(serves 8)

Make a white sauce with 2 sticks oleo or butter, 1 c. flour—cook until it bubbles. Slowlv add 2 c. milk and 1½ t. salt. When sauce boils, remove from heat and pour *onto* 3 beaten egg yolks. Add 1 T. grated onion, 1 8-oz. can mushrooms with juice, 6 c. lobster meat cut in cubes. Cook 2 or 3 minutes and remove from heat. *Last* add ¼ c. sherry. Fill casseroles, top with grated cheese and buttered crumbs. Place under brolier until bubbly. Serve at once.

To cook lobster tails: Plunge 2 lbs. large frozen lobster tails into kettle of rapidly boiling water with 2 T. salt. After water returns to boiling point cook 10 minutes only. Remove all shell and pink membrane—cut in cubes.

FRIED OYSTERS

With a fork beat 1 egg until mixed. Add ½ t. salt, 2 T. flour. Drain 1 pt. extra select oysters in colander. Mix oysters with egg and flour. Only a small amount will cling to the oysters. With a fork lift out one oyster at a time and roll in dried bread crumbs (not cracker crumbs), containing a small amount of flour (1 c. dried bread crumbs to 1 t. flour). Fry in deep fat until *just* brown. Drain on paper towels.

MRS. YOUNG'S SCALLOPED OYSTERS

- 1 qt. oysters
- 1 small box soda crackers
- 1 stick butter
- 1 c. milk
- ½ t. salt

Break crackers into coarse crumbs. In a baking dish place a layer of cracker crumbs. Dot with butter. Cover with oysters, sprinkle with salt, repeat crackers, butter, then oysters. Top baking dish with crumbs. Dot with butter. Add the milk. Cover and cook 15 minutes at 400°. Remove cover and brown.

BAKED RED SNAPPER CREOLE

(serves 8)

Wipe one 6-pound fish with wet paper towel. Be sure that fish is free of scales. Place in greased baking pan. Cover fish with: 1 large onion, sliced; 3 slices breakfast bacon, cubed; 1 bay leaf; 2 t. salt. Bake at 350° for 1 hour. Remove from oven and spread with mustard. Add 1 #2½ can of tomatoes. Bake 30 minutes more.

ANNA'S SHRIMP LOUISIANNE

Sauté until soft, but not brown: ¾ c. oil or butter; 2 medium onions, chopped fine; 2 green peppers, chopped fine. Add: 2 cups tomato juice, ½ cup chicken stock or water. Simmer until tender. Add: 2 c. cooked rice, 2 lbs. cleaned cooked shrimp (5 lbs. in the shell), 1 T. salt, 3 dashes tabasco. Cook all together about 3 minutes. Beat 4 egg yolks. Add 2 c. cream. Just a few minutes before serving add to the shrimp mixture. *Do not allow to boil.*

BARBECUED SHRIMP
(serves 8)

Clean 5 lbs. medium shrimp. Set aside, do not cook. In an iron skillet place: 1 stick oleo or butter; 2 large onions, chopped fine; 2 large garlic cloves, chopped fine. Sauté until yellow. Add: 4 T. curry powder; 2 t. salt; 1 t. grated lemon rind; 6 T. lemon juice; 4 T. soya sauce; 3 T. brown sugar. Cook all together until thick. Add uncooked shrimp and cook 10 minutes. If sauce is too thin, remove shrimp at end of 10 minutes. Boil down sauce. Add shrimp. Serve on steamed rice.

SHRIMP GUMBO

½ c. bacon fat
2 lbs. fresh okra, sliced
(frozen may be used)
1 c. chopped onion
3 pods garlic, chopped

Sauté the above, then add:

3 t. flour
1½ qts. water
1 c. chopped celery
½ c. chopped parsley
½ c. chopped green pepper
2 large bay leaves
12 dashes tabasco sauce
3 T. Lea & Perrins
3 c. tomato puree
1 c. canned tomatoes
3 T. salt

Simmer one hour over low heat. Add 3 lbs. cleaned, raw shrimp (5 lbs. shrimp bought in the shell will be needed). Cook an additional 10 minutes. Serve in soup bowls with border of steamed rice.

SHRIMP RAMEKINS
(serves 4-5)

Cook 1 lb. of peeled deveined medium-size shrimp 10 minutes in boiling water with 2 t. salt. Hard boil 2 eggs and slice. Place sliced hard-boiled eggs in bottom of the ramekins, fill with the shrimp mixture, top with buttered crumbs. Brown in 350° oven.

Shrimp mixture: Sauté 3 T. chopped onion in 2 T. melted oleo until soft. Add 1½ t. flour and cook 2 minutes. Add 1 4-oz. can of mushrooms with juice, and ½ can concentrated mushroom soup, 1 c. evaporated milk, ½ t. salt, ¼ t. dry mustard, ¼ c. sliced ripe olives, and the cooked shrimp. Remove from heat and add ¼ c. sherry.

Note: If shrimp in the shell are used, about 2 lbs. will be needed to equal 1 lb. shelled and deveined shrimp.

CHAPTER XIV

SOUPS

CRAB BISQUE

CREAM OF CORN SOUP

CREAM OF POTATO SOUP

CREAM MONGALE

VAN DUZOR ONION SOUP

CHAPTER XIV

SOUPS

Recipes

CRAB BISQUE

1 tall can evaporated milk	1/8 t. mace
2 c. water mixed with	2 t. salt
2 t. flour	⅓ lb. crab meat

Place all of the above ingredients in the top of a double boiler. Cook over hot water 20 minutes. Stir occasionally. When ready to serve add 3 T. sherry.

CREAM OF CORN SOUP

(serves 4-5)

1 #2½ can cream style yellow corn, 1 c. hot water—Allow to boil 2 minutes. Press through a coarse sieve. Place in top of double boiler. Add: 1 tall can evaporated milk, 1 T. flour and 1 t. salt, mixed with 1 c. water, 2 T. grated onion. Cook over hot water 20 minutes. Stir occasionally.

CREAM OF POTATO SOUP

1 large potato, peeled and sliced
1 medium onion, peeled and sliced
1 c. boiling water

Cook until potato is soft. Put through a coarse sieve.

Add:	½ t. celery seed
1 tall can evaporated milk	1 T. salt
2 T. chopped parsley	1 T. butter

Cook in double boiler about 10 minutes.

CREAM MONGALE SOUP

1 can tomato soup	1 t. Lea & Perrins
1 can pea soup	1 c. evaporated milk
2¼ c. water	¼ c. sherry
1 t. sugar	½ t. salt

Mix all together except the sherry. When it comes to a boil and is smooth, remove from heat and add the sherry.

VAN DUZOR ONION SOUP

1 large onion, sliced, 2 c. water—Place in top of double boiler. Cook over direct heat about 10 minutes. In a fruit jar place 1 T. flour, ½ c. water, 1 t. salt. Shake until smooth. Pour the hot onion mixture into the flour mixture, return all to the top of the double boiler, place over hot water. Add 1 tall can evaporated milk, 1 T. butter. Cook 15 minutes. Serve soup in bowls with a square of toast and 2 T. grated Parmesan cheese on top.

CHAPTER XV

VEGETABLES

Em's Almond Brown Rice
Baked Potatoes Lawrence
Candied Sweet Potatoes
Carrots a la Hungary
Corn Pudding
Corn Okra Jambalaya
Creamed Chestnuts
Duchess Potatoes
Dutch Red Cabbage
Mashed Baked Sweet Potatoes
Potato Puffs
Potatoes au gratin
Red Rice
Sautéed Corn
Scalloped Egg Plant
Scalloped Potatoes
Scalloped Sweet Potatoes and Apples
Scalloped Summer Squash
Scalloped Fresh Tomatoes
Spanish Green Lima Beans
Spanish Egg Plant
Spinach Au Gratin
Spinach with Egg Dressing
Sweet Potato and Pineapple Scallop
Sweet Potato Pone
Squash Souffle
French Fried Egg Plant

CHAPTER XV

VEGETABLES

EM'S ALMOND BROWN RICE

(serves 8)

Brown together in a large sauce pan:

1 pkg. vermicelli (8 oz.), broken in very small pieces (¼ inch)
1 stick butter or oleo

Add:
1 c. uncooked rice which has been well washed
1½ c. consommé or chicken stock
1½ c. water
1 t. salt

Cover tightly and simmer over low heat for 20 minutes without stirring (or until liquid has been absorbed). Turn into a greased baking dish (2 qt.). Cover with sliced or slivered almonds. Bake until nuts are brown (about 20 minutes).

BAKED POTATO LAWRENCE

(serves 6)

1 c. sour cream, whipped
2 t. grated onion juice
1 t. salt

After potatoes are baked, score and spoon 4 T. of cream into each potato.

CANDIED SWEET POTATOES

6 medium sweet potatoes
½ c. brown sugar
¼ c. water
½ stick oleo or butter
½ t. salt
Grated rind of half a lemon or orange

Peel potatoes and cut in half crosswise. Place in greased baking dish. Mix remaining ingredients and pour over potatoes. Cover and bake at 350° for 1 hour. Uncover to brown. Potatoes are better if not crowded in baking dish.

CARROTS A LA HUNGARY

1 bunch raw carrots—Wash, scrape, cut in 3-inch sticks. Place in sauce pan, add ½ c. *boiling* water and ¼ t. salt. Cook until tender and drain. Mix: ¼ c. vinegar, ⅔ c. sugar, 1 T. butter. Add the carrot sticks and simmer over low heat for 10 minutes. Add ¼ c. chopped parsley a minute before serving.

CORN PUDDING

(serves 6)

5 ears corn, grated (or 2 small boxes frozen cream style corn)
3 c. milk
4 eggs
2 t. salt
1 T. butter

Beat eggs slightly. Mix all ingredients together. Pour into greased baking dish. Set dish in pan of cold water. Bake at 325° for 1½ hours. Caution: If water around pudding should begin to boil add cold water or pudding will be watery.

CORN OKRA JAMBALAYA

(serves 6)

¼ lb. bacon fried until crisp. Remove from pan. In bacon fat sauté: 1 lb. of okra, sliced; 2 medium onions, chopped. Cook to seal the okra but *do not brown.* Add tomatoes from #303 can. Cook 5 minutes. Add corn cut from 3 ears of corn and 1½ t. salt. Cook 5 minutes more. *Must not be runny*. Place in greased baking dish. Sprinkle with chinese noodles and crisp bacon, crushed. Bake in oven 10 minutes.

For the best jambalaya, use fresh corn only.

CREAMED CHESTNUTS

(serves 10)

Chestnuts are difficult to shell. The most successful method: Score chestnuts on the flat side. Place in a shallow pan with 1 stick oleo for 5 lbs. chestnuts. Bake at 400° for 30 minutes. Peel while hot.

In a double boiler make a thin white sauce of: 2 T. butter, 2 T. flour, 1 t. salt. Cook until it bubbles, add 2 c. milk, cook 10 minutes. Add 5 lbs. of shelled chestnuts and continue cooking 10 minutes longer. Chestnuts will be sufficiently cooked. This can be used as a vegetable at Thanksgiving.

DUCHESS POTATOES

(serves 6-8)

Place 1 qt. mashed potatoes (either cold or hot) in electric mixer. Add 6 egg yolks and ½ t. salt. Beat until well blended. If not left over mashed potatoes, add 2 T. butter and additional ½ t. salt. Fold in 6 beaten egg whites. Bake at 350° for 30 minutes.

DUTCH RED CABBAGE

(serves 6)

1 large head red cabbage, shredded
1 small white potato, peeled and sliced thin
4 apples, peeled and sliced
½ c. sugar
½ c. vinegar
½ c. water
1 t. salt
2 T. bacon or ham fat

Place potato in the bottom of a large aluminum pot. Add half cabbage, cover with half of the apples. Repeat. Add remaining ingredients. Cover. Cook slowly for 2½ hours. Stir occasionally. This is the only vegetable we know that requires such lengthy cooking.

MASHED BAKED SWEET POTATOES

(serves 6)

3 lbs. sweet potatoes (boiled peeled, and mashed)
⅓ stick butter or oleo
⅓ c. sugar
1 t. salt
1 t. vanilla
2 t. grated orange or lemon rind
⅓ c. orange juice

Combine all ingredients. Place in greased baking pan, bake 30 minutes at 350°.

POTATO PUFFS

(serves 6-8)

1 qt. mashed potatoes (may be left-over potatoes)
1¼ c. flour
2 t. baking powder
½ t. salt
3 eggs (well beaten)
½ c. milk

Mix in the above order. Drop by small spoonfuls into deep fat at 365°. Remove from fat as soon as brown, drain on crushed paper toweling. Serve at once, or keep warm in the oven.

POTATOES AU GRATIN

(serves 6)

Peel 5 large potatoes, cut in cubes. Place in briskly boiling water with 1 t. salt. Boil until tender and drain. Pour into a 2 qt. baking dish and cover with the following sauce: 4 T. flour; 4 T. butter or oleo. Cook until it bubbles. Add 2 c. milk. Stir until the sauce boils. Remove from heat and add: 1 c. grated sharp cheese, stir until melted. Add 1 t. salt. Cover the top with buttered dry bread crumbs. Bake at 350° until brown, about 20 to 30 minutes.

RED RICE

(serves 8)

2 c. rice, washed and drained until dry
1 #2 can tomatoes
1 t. Lea & Perrins
1 t. salt
1 medium onion, chopped
1 green pepper, chopped
2 T. curry powder
2 T. bacon fat

Sauté onion, pepper, curry powder in bacon fat 3 minutes. Do not brown. Mix all ingredients, place in top of double boiler over direct low heat. Cook 10 minutes. Place over boiling water, steam until tender. It may be necessary to add additional tomato juice, ½ c. at the time. Delicious to use in ring mold filled with a creamed meat or fish.

For ring: When rice is tender grease ring mold, add rice, press down gently. Place plate on top, keep hot until serving time. Turn out on hot chop plate. Fill center with any desired creamed mixture.

SAUTÉED CORN

(serves 6)

6 ears of corn (well filled out, but not hard)
3 T. bacon or ham fat
1 c. water
1 t. salt

Shuck corn and remove silks with brush. With a potato peeler or very sharp knife, cut just the tops from the rows of corn. With a dull knife, scrape out the creamy part, leaving the tough fibre on the cob. Place bacon or ham fat in heavy skillet. When heated, add corn with water and salt. Cover. Stir occasionally. This should cook down to almost the consistancy of mush. Cooking time: about 30 minutes. If too dry, add a small amount of water. This is a real favorite in the Deep South.

SCALLOPED EGG PLANT

(serves 4-5)

1 medium egg plant
½ small onion, chopped
1 small green pepper, chopped
2 T. bacon fat
3 T. dry bread crumbs
½ t. salt
1 egg, well beaten
½ t. Lea & Perrins

Peel egg plant, slice, place in pot of *boiling* water. Cook until tender (about 15 minutes). Drain in a colander, mash. Sauté pepper and onion in fat. Add to the mashed egg plant. Also, add the seasoning and bread crumbs. Pour into greased 1 qt. baking pan. Cover with buttered crumbs. Bake at 375° for 30 minutes. This should brown on top and fluff up.

SCALLOPED POTATOES
(serves 6)

3 lbs. potatoes, before peeling
1 pt. of very thin white sauce
1 T. oleo or butter
1 T. flour
2 t. salt
1 pt. milk

Peel potatoes and slice very thin. Arrange in 2 qt. baking pan. Pour white sauce over potatoes and add 1 T. melted butter. Place cover on pan and bake at 350° until sauce begins to boil. Remove cover and continue baking until potatoes are tender. Full baking time, about 2 hours. Immediately upon removing potatoes from oven, add 2 T. milk over all.

SCALLOPED SWEET POTATOES AND APPLES
(serves 5-6)

2 lbs. sweet potatoes (about 5)
⅓ c. brown sugar
½ t. salt
1 lb. apples (about 3)
3 T. melted butter or oleo

Scrub potatoes, do not peel. Cook in boiling water until *partly* done. Peel, slice. Place half potatoes in baking dish. Cover with one-half peeled, cored, sliced apples. Sprinkle with salt and sugar. Repeat. Add melted butter or oleo, also, juice of one lemon. Bake at 350° for 1 hour.

SCALLOPED SUMMER SQUASH
(serves 6-8)

Wash and slice 2 lbs. squash. Cook 5 minutes in boiling water. Drain in a colander. Sauté in 1 T. bacon fat, ½ green pepper, sliced and 1 medium onion, sliced. Drain 1 4-oz. can mushrooms, save juice. Mix lightly squash, pepper, onion, mushrooms, and 1 t. salt. Place half of the mixture in a baking dish. Mix 1 can mushroom soup with juice from whole mushrooms. Spoon half over the squash. Repeat. Top with grated cheese and buttered crumbs. Bake 30 minutes at 350°.

SCALLOPED FRESH TOMATOES
(serves 6)

3 lbs. *very* ripe tomatoes
2 t. salt
3 T. sugar
4 T. melted butter or oleo
2 c. coarse bread crumbs (soft)

Pour boiling water over tomatoes. Skin and slice. Place half the tomatoes in baking dish. Sprinkle with salt and sugar and crumbs. Repeat and sprinkle top crumbs with the melted butter or oleo. Bake at 350° for 1 hour. Unless tomatoes are fully ripe, the product will not be satisfactory.

SPANISH GREEN LIMA BEANS

(serves 6)

Sauté:
½ c. chopped celery
1 T. chopped onion
½ garlic clove in
4 t. ham or bacon fat
Add:
4 t. flour
Stir until it bubbles.

Add:
1 c. milk
1 t. salt
1 T. chopped pimento
1 8-oz. can mushrooms with juice
1 10-oz. box frozen green lima beans which have been cooked in small amount of salted water (boiling).

Allow to simmer 10 minutes, before serving. This is especially suited to the chafing dish.

SPANISH EGG PLANT

(serves 6)

2 lbs. egg plant
½ medium onion, chopped
1 green pepper, chopped
1 T. bacon or ham fat
¾ c. tomato puree
1 c. cheese, grated
½ t. salt

In a large sauce pan sauté green pepper and onion in bacon fat 3 minutes. Add egg plant, peeled and diced. Cover, cook for 15 minutes. When egg plant is tender add tomato puree and allow to cook down so that it is not watery. Add salt. Reduce heat to a minimum. Add cheese and stir until the ingredients are blended.

SPINACH AU GRATIN

(serves 6)

¼ lb. sliced bacon
1 10-oz. box frozen chopped spinach
1 egg (slightly beaten)
1 c. milk
½ t. salt
¾ c. Parmesan cheese
½ c. soft bread crumbs

Dice bacon and fry until partly done. Remove from pan. Cook spinach according to directions on package. Drain thoroughly. To beaten egg, add 1 T. bacon fat, milk, salt, spinach, bread crumbs and ½ of the cheese. Pour mixture into 1 qt. baking pan. Cover with bacon and remaining cheese. Sprinkle with paprika. Bake 30 minutes in 350° oven.

SPINACH WITH EGG DRESSING

(serves 6-8)

2 10-oz. boxes frozen chopped spinach. Boil 10 minutes in ½ c. water with 1 t. salt. Drain. Add the following dressing. Mix lightly and serve hot.

Dressing:

- 2 hard boiled eggs, chopped fine
- 3 strips bacon, fried until crisp, drained and crumbled
- Fat from the fried bacon
- 1 T. mayonnaise
- ½ t. grated onion
- ½ t. salt

SWEET POTATOES AND PINEAPPLE SCALLOP

- 3 lbs. sweet potatoes (about 6)
- 1 #2 can crushed pineapple
- ½ c. brown sugar (packed)
- ⅓ lb. breakfast bacon, cut in cubes
- ½ t. salt

Partly cook the cubed bacon. Boil potatoes without peeling. When tender, drain, peel, mash. Add drained crushed pineapple, brown sugar, salt. Place in baking pan, top with partly cooked, cubed breakfast bacon. Bake at 350° until top browns, about 30 minutes.

SWEET POTATO PONE

(serves 6-8)

- 1 qt. grated or ground raw sweet potatoes
- 1 egg, beaten
- ⅔ c. cane syrup
- ½ stick butter or oleo
- 1½ c. milk
- ½ c. flour
- ½ t. grated nutmeg
- 1 t. ground cinnamon
- ½ t. salt
- grated rind of 1 orange

Sift together all dry ingredients. Mix with potato and all other ingredients. Pour into 2 qt. baking dish. Bake 2½ hours at 300°. Stir every 30 minutes. The last hour do not stir, allow to brown. If pone appears too dry, add ½ c. milk during the baking. Originally, in the Deep South, this usually accompanied game.

SQUASH SOUFFLE

(serves 6)

- 1 c. thick white sauce (see sauces)
- 3 egg yolks, beaten
- 3 egg whites, beaten stiff
- 2 c. mashed squash
- ½ t. salt
- ½ t. onion juice

Combine all ingredients, and last, fold in beaten egg whites. Pour into greased baking dish. Bake 30 minutes at 350°.

FRENCH FRIED EGG PLANT

Peel medium sized egg plant. Cut in strips (as for French fried potatoes). Place in cold water to prevent discoloration. Drain thoroughly, dry on paper towels. Beat slightly 1 egg with 1 T. water. Mix: 2 c. dried bread crumbs (not cracker crumbs), 2 T. flour, 1 T. salt. Dip egg plant strips in egg mixture, then in bread crumbs. Fry in deep fat until brown.

CHAPTER XVI

MISCELLANEOUS

SOUTHERN CORN BREAD STUFFING FOR:

DUCKS

CHICKENS

PORK CHOPS

TURKEYS

BAKED BANANAS

PEACH CHUTNEY

SPICED SUGARED NUTS

CINNAMON APPLE SLICES

ENGLISH YORKSHIRE PUDDING

CHAPTER XVI

MISCELLANEOUS

Recipes

SOUTHERN CORN BREAD STUFFING FOR:

DUCKS
CHICKENS
PORK CHOPS
TURKEYS

2 c. cold corn bread
2 c. stale bread (biscuits, rolls or loaf)
½ c. chopped celery
¼ c. chopped onion
1 t. sage, rubbed
½ t. salt
½ t. celery seed
3 T. chopped parsley
3 T. bacon fat or ham fat or oleo

Mix all together well and add just enough boiling water or stock to make a crumbly mixture, about ½ - 1 c. Spoon lightly into the fowl. Double this recipe for a turkey.

BAKED BANANAS

In a baking pan, place:

8 large bananas (cut in half crosswise)
½ t. salt
Juice of ½ lemon
¼ c. sugar
NO WATER

Cover and bake at 350° until liquid in pan boils. Remove cover. Bake until tender, about 30 minutes.

PEACH CHUTNEY (TO SERVE WITH CURRIED DISHES)
(about 4 qts.)

2 c. chopped onion
1 lb. white raisins
2 cloves garlic, chopped
8 lbs. peaches, cut in quarters
3 T. red chili powder
½ c. crystallized ginger, chopped
4 T. mustard seed
2 T. salt
2 qts. apple cider vinegar
3 lbs. sugar

Mix all together except peaches. Simmer 1½ hours, adding fruit last half hour. Pears can be used instead of peaches. Pour into jars while hot and seal.

SPICED SUGARED NUTS

1 c. white sugar
1 c. brown sugar
¼ c. water
1 t. ground cinnamon
½ t. nutmeg
1 t. salt
1 lb. shelled pecans

Mix water, sugar, spices. Add nuts, cook over medium heat, stir constantly until pot is dry. Pour onto wax paper and separate immediately.

CINNAMON APPLE SLICES

(serves 6)

Wash and core 4 apples. Cut in thick slices, about 3 or 4 to each apple. Place slices on cookie sheet. Sprinkle with ⅓ c. sugar mixed with ½ t. cinnamon and ½ t. salt. Cover with another cookie sheet. Cook 10 minutes or until tender. Uncover to brown lightly. Serve 3 or 4 with pork roast or baked ham croquettes.

ENGLISH YORKSHIRE PUDDING (TO SERVE WITH ROAST BEEF)

(serves 8-10)

1½ c. sifted flour
1 t. salt
3 c. milk
6 eggs

Beat whole eggs until very light. To the flour and salt add the milk very slowly using a wire whip. When free of lumps, add eggs. Spoon 3 T. roast beef drippings into baking pan and while hot pour in the pudding mixture. Bake at 350° for 30 minutes. Baste 2 or 3 times with beef drippings. This will rise at first, but fall some before it is done. Cut immediately in 3 or 4 inch squares and serve hot with roast beef.

CHAPTER XVII

NEW RECIPES

CASSELL'S EGG PLANT

CHICKEN ADELE

OUR BAKED ROAST BEEF HASH

STRAWBERRY CHARLOTTE

CARDINAL SALAD

CHUTNEY

RICE CHEESE CASSEROLE

BLUEBERRY ICE BOX PIE

CHAPTER XVII

NEW RECIPES

CASSELL'S EGG PLANT

(serves 4)

One medium eggplant. Peel, slice in small thin pieces and soak 30 minutes in salted water (1 T. salt) to cover. Place plate on top to keep eggplant under water. Drain. Sauté eggplant lightly in 2 t. bacon fat or olive oil, add 1 clove chopped garlic. Do not brown. Place in pyrex pie pan. Mix ½ 8-oz. can spaghetti sauce with 3 T. water. Pour over eggplant. Cover with Parmesan cheese. Bake at 350° until it bubbles.

CHICKEN ADELE

1 qt. cooked diced chicken
1 pt. soft diced bread cubes
1 T. grated onion
2 c. chicken broth
⅓ c. chopped parsley
3 eggs, beaten
1 t. Lea & Perrins sauce
salt and pepper to taste

Mix all together lightly. Place in greased square baking pan. Cover with crushed corn flakes, then chopped toasted almonds. Dribble melted butter over the top. Bake 30 minutes at 350° or until firm.

SAUCE

1 can condensed mushroom soup
1 t. grated onion
1 4-oz. can mushrooms with juice
1 small can evaporated milk
water to make the right consistency

Simmer 5 minutes. Cut chicken in squares and spoon sauce over each serving.

OUR BAKED ROAST BEEF HASH

(serves 8-10)

6 medium potatoes, boiled, peeled, and sliced
2 qts. meat from roast, ground with coarse grinder
1 T. Lea & Perrins sauce
3 dashes Tabasco
2 c. water
2 medium onions, chopped

Mix lightly. Taste for salt. Place in greased baking pan. Bake 30 minutes at 350°. Serve with mustard pickle.

STRAWBERRY CHARLOTTE
(serves 6)

Soak together for 5 minutes:
- 1½ T. plain gelatin
- ¼ C. cold water

Add:
- ¼ c. boiling water
- 2 T. sugar
- ⅛ t. salt

Chill mixture until it begins to thicken. Gradually add 1 pt. strawberries, fresh or frozen (thawed). Fold in ¾ c. heavy cream whipped. Beat 1 egg white, add 2 T. sugar, and fold in last. Spoon into flat pan. Refrigerate at least 2 hours. Cut in squares; serve with strawberries over it.

CARDINAL SALAD

- 2 boxes lemon jello
- 2 c. boiling water
- ⅔ c. beet juice
- ⅔ c. vinegar
- 1½ t. salt
- ¼ c. (frozen) horseradish
- 1 c. chopped celery
- 2 c. chopped beets
- 2 T. sugar
- 2 t. onion juice

Dissolve jello in hot water, add all ingredients except beets and celery. Chill until liquid begins to thicken. Add beets and celery and pour into molds.

CHUTNEY (with a new base)
(about 4 qts.)

- 1 pkg. dried peaches
  soak in water 30 minutes, peel, and cut in half
- 2 #2 cans sliced apples

Prepare spices with vinegar, etc., as for peach chutney (see p. 111). Cook 20 minutes, add apples and dried peaches. Cook until thick. Pour into sterile jars.

RICE CHEESE CASSEROLE

(serves 8)

2 c. rice, cooked
2 c. grated yellow cheese
1 c. chopped parsley
2 green onions chopped *or* 4 T. grated onion
½ clove garlic, chopped
1 t. salt
½ c. salad oil
2 c. milk

Sauté onion and garlic in salad oil. Do not brown. Mix all ingredients. Bake in 2-qt. casserole at 350° for 45 minutes.

BLUEBERRY ICE BOX PIE

(9-inch pie)

1 can condensed milk
3 T. lemon juice
1 #303 can of blueberries
⅛ t. salt

Drain berries—reserve the juice. Place milk and lemon juice in electric mixer and beat until quite thick. Add salt. Fold in berries. Pour into graham cracker crust. Refrigerate two hours. Boil down juice to a syrup. Chill. To serve, cover pie with unsweetened whipped cream and dribble juice over the top.

Presidents of the University Club

1947	Jefferson J. Coleman
1948	Burton R. Morley
1949	Thomas G. Andrews
1950	James B. McMillan
1951	J. Henry Walker
1952	James M. Faircloth
1953	Ernest G. Williams
1954	Henry H. Hale
1955	John F. Ramsey
1956	Eric Rodgers
1957	William D. Jordan
1958	Kenneth W. Coons
1959	M. Torrey Jemison
1960	T. Earle Johnson
1961	Lovic P. Hodnette
1962	Tom S. Birdsong
1963	Eugene H. Price
1964	L. Tennent Lee Jr.
1965	Philip E. LaMoreaux
1966	Clarence T. Sharpton
1967	William E. Pickens Jr.
1968	Joseph E. Lane Jr.
1969	Norman M. Agnew Jr.
1970	T. Walter Oliver
1971	Clark O. Thornton
1972	John C. Seymour
1973	John P. Hansen
1974	Marion J. Posey
1975	Charles R. Estes
1976	William K. Rey
1977	Edward H. Moseley

1978	Marvin T. Ormond
1979	Myrtis W. Gordon
1980	Vann Waldrop
1981	Glenda K. Guyton
1982	Bernard J. Sloan
1983	Douglas E. Jones
1984	Wilma S. Greene
1985	Morris L. Mayer
1986	David Cole
1987	Frederic Goossen
1988	Randolph M. Fowler
1989	MarLa S. Sayers
1990	Robert Haubein
1991	Jerry C. Oldshue
1992	Robert Shaw
1993	Judith Bonner
1994	Claude Burns
1995	Lynne April
1996	E.. Calhoun Wilson
1997	Kathleen Randall Cramer
1998	John Murdock
1999	Pam Parker
2000	Jim Johnson
2001	Hattie Kaufman
2002	E. Calhoun Wilson
2003	Charles Hilburn
2004	Tom Jones
2005	E. Calhoun Wilson
2006	David Nelson
2007	David Nelson
2008	Glenda K. Guyton
2009	Glenda K. Guyton

Index

**Index to the recipes, by name of dish:*

Afternoon Tea Dainties, 29
Alline's Jellied Fruit Salad, 77
Almond Macaroon Pudding, 37
Angel Charlotte, 37
Angel Food, 17
Anna's Shrimp Louisianne, 93
Apple Crisp, 38
Apple Spice Muffins, 10
Apricot Bavarian Cream, 38
Avocado Dream Salad, 77

Baked Bananas, 111
Baked Ham Croquettes, 52
Baked Pork Chops a la Marjorie, 54
Baked Potato Lawrence, 101
Baked Red Snapper Creole, 93
Baltimore Crab Cakes, 91
Banana Cake, 17
Barbecue Sauce (Red), 88
Barbecued Shrimp, 94
Best White Fruit Cake, 17
Bethel's Shortcake, 42
Black and White Layer Cake, 18
Blueberry Ice Box Pie, 117
Blueberry Tarts, 64
Bombay Sauce for Chicken Breast, 88
Bran Muffins, 10
Bread Crumb Griddle Cakes, 8
Broiled Chicken, 69
Broiled Chicken Marjorie, 69
Butter Fingers, 29
Butterscotch Pudding, 39
Butterscotch Sauce, 85
Butterscotch Tarts, 64

Candied Sweet Potatoes, 101
Caramel Baked Custard, 38
Caramel Party Cake, 18
Cardinal Salad, 116
Carrots a la Hungary, 101
Cassell's Egg Plant, 115
Charlotte Russe, 39
Cheese Ball, 25
Cheese Fondue, 25
Cheese Pie, 25
Cheese Ramekins, 25
Cheese Souffle, 26
Cheesey Apple Pie, 59
Chewy Chocolate Squares or Brownies, 29
Chicken Adele, 115
Chicken Breast Almondine, 70
Chicken Brunswick Stew, 71
Chicken Continental, 71
Chicken Divan, 71
Chicken Hash, 71
Chicken Hawaiian, 72
Chicken Livers with Pineapple and Almonds, 72
Chicken Salad, 77
Chicken Tetrazinni, 72
Chocolate Chiffon Pie, 62
Chocolate Chip Almond Pie, 60
Chocolate Coconut Drop Cookies, 30
Chocolate Crumb Pudding, 35
Chocolate Fudge Pudding, 35
Chocolate Icing, 20
Chocolate Roll, 35
Chocolate Sauce, 85
Chocolate Souffle, 36
Chocolate Tarts, 64
Chutney, 116

Cinnamon Apple Slices, 112
Cinnamon Rolls, 12
Cocktail Sauce, 86
Coconut Cream Tarts, 64
Cole Slaw Deluxe, 78
Cooked Salad Dressing, 82
Corn Bread (Muffins or Sticks), 8
Corn Okra Jambalaya, 102
Corn Pudding, 102
Country Salad, 78
Cousin Cora's Chocolate Ice Box Pudding, 36
Crab a la Newburg, 91
Crab Bisque, 97
Crab Cakes au Gratin, 91
Crab Gumbo, 91
Crab Noodle Casserole, 92
Crab Salad, 79
Cranberry Salad, 79
Cream of Corn Soup, 97
Cream of Potato Soup, 97
Cream Mongale Soup, 97
Creamed Chestnuts, 102
Creamed Chicken and Mushrooms, 73
Crescents, 29
Cucumber Salad, 79
Curried Lamb, 53
Cut Biscuits, 7

Date Bars, 30
Date Graham Cracker Meringue, 40
Date Ice Box Roll, 39
Date Nut Angel Pudding, 39
Date Scones, 11
De Luxe Chocolate Cake Filling, 20
Deep Dish Apple Pie, 60
Deviled Crab, 92
Deviled Eggs, 47
Devils Food Cake, 18
Devil's Food Cake de Luxe, 18
Different Sauce for Pork, 86
Dinner Rolls, 11
Drop Biscuits, 7
Drop Cookies, 30
Duchess Potatoes, 102
Dutch Red Cabbage, 103

Egg Bread, 8
Eggnog Pie, *see* Rum Chiffon Pie
Eggs Concordia, 47
Eleanora's White Cake, 19
Em's Almond Brown Rice, 101
English Yorkshire Pudding, 112

Flower Garden Cake, 39
Fool-Proof White Icing, 21
French Dressing, 82
French Fried Egg Plant, 108
Fried Oysters, 93
Frozen Fruit Salad for 12, 78
Frozen Fudge Pie, 60
Fruit Filling, 21
Fudge Pie, 36

Glazed Strawberry Pie, 60
Glorified Pudding, 40
Gold Cake, 19
Goldenrod Eggs, 47
Graham Cracker Crust Mix, 59

Ham, How We Bake, 51
Ham a la King, 52
Ham Timables, 52
Hard Sauce, 86
Heavenly Pie, 40
Hot Fruit Toddy, 3
Hot Mince Tarts, 65
Hot Potato Salad, 79
Hot Russian Tea, 3
Hot Spiced Tomato Juice, 4

Japanese Spice Cake, 19
Jellied Lamb Mold, 53
Jessie's Peach Krinkle, 42

Kappa Punch (Mock Champagne), 3
Kate's Christmas Salad, 80

Lady Baltimore Angel Cake Filling, 21
Lamb Leg, How to Bake a, 51
Lemon Crunch Dessert, 41
Lemon Filling, 21
Lemon Tarts, 65
Lettuce Roquefort, 81
Liver Cakes, 54
Lobster Thermidor, 92
Louise's Chicken Aspic, 80

Margaret's Chocolate Pie, 62
Marguerites, 31
Marion's Jellied Mock Chicken Loaf, 55
Mary's Cheese Straws, 26
Mary's Lemon Pie, 62
Mary Ann's Coconut Cookies, 30
Mashed Baked Sweet Potatoes, 103
Mayonnaise, 82
Meringue Shells or Kisses, 30
Minted Pineapple Sauce for Ice Cream, 85
Mock Hollandaise Sauce (for Vegetables), 88
Mrs. Rainer's Punch for 100, 3
Mrs. Young's Scalloped Oysters, 93
Mustard Beans (Cold Salad), 80

Nut Bread, 9

Old Fashioned Chicken Pie, 73
Orange Cream Shortcake, 41
Orange-Fruit Nut Bread, 9
Orange Rolls, 11
Orange Sauce, 9
Orange Sauce for Gingerbread, 85
Orange Suzettes, 9
Orange Toast, 13
Our Baked Roast Beef Hash, 115
"Our" Salisbury Steak, 54
Oven Fried Chicken — Parmesan, 73

Pastries and Shells, 59
Peach Chutney, 111
Peach Melba de Bouffant, 42
Peanut Butter Drop Biscuits, 7
Pecan Pie, 61
Pecan Squares, 31
Peppermint Chiffon Pie, 63
Peter Pans, 31
Pie Shells, 59
Pimento Cheese Squares, 26
Pineapple Crunch Cake, 20
Pineapple Drop Biscuits, 7
Pineapple Ice Box Dessert, 42
Pineapple Tarts, 65
Pirates Lime Pie, 63
Plain Muffins, 10
Plum Glazed Cheese Pie, 61
Porcupines, 53
Pot Roast at Its Best, 51
Potato Puffs, 103
Potatoes au Gratin, 103
Puffy Omelet, 47
Punch for 30, 4
Punch for 100 (with sherbet), 4

Quick Caramel Frosting, 22

Raisin Bread, 10
Raisin Sauce for Ham and Tongue, 87
Raspberry or Strawberry Chiffon Pie, 63
Red Barbecued Chicken, 69
Red Raspberry Cream Pie, 61
Red Rice, 104
Refrigerator Rolls, 11
Rena Madge's Chess Pie, 61
Rice Cheese Casserole, 117
Roberta's Lemon Ice Box Pie, 62
Rum Chiffon Pie or Eggnog Pie, 63

Sallie's Cheese Waters for Tea, 26
Sallie's Chocolate Ice Box Dessert, 37
Sallie's Macaroon Pie, 41
Sauce Champignon (for Chicken), 86
Sauce Remoulade (for Shrimp), 86
Sautéed Chicken Breast, 70
Sautéed Chicken Breast — Bombay Sauce, 70

Sautéed Chicken Breast with Sauce Champignon, 70
Sautéed Corn, 104
Scalloped Egg Plant, 104
Scalloped Fresh Tomatoes, 105
Scalloped Potatoes, 105
Scalloped Summer Squash, 105
Scalloped Sweet Potatoes and Apples, 105
Scotch Shortbread, 31
Sea Foam Frosting, 22
Shrimp Gumbo, 94
Shrimp Ramekins, 94
Shrimp Salad, 81
Sour Cream Cake, 19
Sour Cream Sauce (for Steamed Cabbage), 86
Southern Corn Bread Stuffing, 111
Spanish Egg Plant, 106
Spanish Green Lima Beans, 106
Spanish Omelet Sauce, 87
Spiced Sugared Nuts, 112
Spinach au Gratin, 106
Spinach with Egg Dressing, 107
Spoon Bread, 8
Spritz, 31
Squash Souffle, 107
Strawberry Charlotte, 116
Strawberry Chiffon Pie, *see* Raspberry Chiffon Pie
Stuffed Baked Pork Chops, 54
Sunday Toast, 13
Supreme Sauce (for Broccoli, Cauliflower, etc.), 87
Swedish Limpl, 12
Swedish Tea Ring, 12
Sweet Potato Pone, 107
Sweet Potatoes and Pineapple Scallop, 107
Syllabub for a Party, 43

Tangerine Sauce for Roast Duck, 87
Tart Shells, 59
Tartare Sauce (for Fried Sea Foods), 88
Texas Barbecue Sauce (for Half Chicken or Pork Chops), 88
Texas Barbecued Chicken, 69
Thousand Island Dressing, 82
Tipsy Pudding, 43
Toasted Rolls for Luncheon, 13
Tomato Aspic, 81
Tomato French Dressing, 82
Tossed Salads, 81

University Club Summer Special, 55
Upsidedown Date Pudding, 43

Van Duzor Onion Soup, 98
Virginia's Molded Chicken Salad, 81

Welsh Rabbit, 26
White Sauce (Medium), 87
Wine Sauce, 85
Woodstock, 53